1952

WHAT A YEAR TO BE BORN!

Written by
Robin Bennett-Freebairn and Joe Toussaint

Published by Emersive
www.whatayeartobeborn.com

C000183437

What happened in 1952? We have a special affinity for the year we were born, but how much do we really know about it? This guide takes you through the highs and lows of an historic year in the midst of the baby boom generation. The colour-coded chapters unlock a wealth of information that brings you closer to what life was like in this milestone year.

Contents

▶ Introduction

1952 saw the death of a much beloved King, George VI, and the ascension to the throne of Queen Elizabeth II. Britain was still recovering from the ravages of war and bomb sites still littered our towns and cities. Whilst rationing had eased, there were still restrictions on the purchasing of tea and sugar. The country was once again governed by wartime Prime Minister Winston Churchill. Across the pond in America, Harry S. Truman stepped down and was replaced by World War Two general Dwight D. Eisenhower. The shackles of wartime were further loosened when, at home, the Prime Minister announced the abolition of the identity card. Many lost their lives in a freak weather event at Lynmouth, North Devon and scores died at a horrific railway disaster at Harrow and Wealdstone on the outskirts of London.

The first music charts in the UK were published by the New Musical Express magazine and Al Martino's *Here in My Heart* was crowned the first number one. There were also hits for the forces' sweetheart Vera Lynn and the newly founded Billy Haley and the Comets, the latter heralding the birth of rock and roll. Television was in its infancy and infants were well catered for. Sooty and Bill and Ben both debuted on our small screens. In the cinema, audiences were treated to a mixture of wartime dramas such as *Angels One Five*, crime in the shape of *Blind Man's Bluff* and comedy from the Goons, Peter Sellers et al, in *Down Among the Z Men*. In America, Marilyn Monroe was truly on the treadmill, churning out five movies with mixed results. The most enduring film of the year was the tense western *High Noon*, starring Gary Cooper as the redoubtable Marshal Will Kane. In literature two books were published which coincidentally happened to later be turned into two of the three films that James Dean starred in in his short career, namely John Steinbeck's *East of Eden* and Edna Ferber's *Giant*.

In world news, the newly independent India held its first general election where Pandit Nehru's Congress Party secured victory. A 9.0 magnitude earthquake hit the Kamchatka Peninsula in Eastern Russia, sending a tsunami out into the Pacific, leaving thousands dead. The British Empire was in decline and there were major uprisings in Egypt and Kenya.

In sport Manchester United won the football league and Newcastle United the F.A. Cup. The Winter and Summer Olympics both took place in Scandinavia. The combined gold medal tally for Great Britain from the Oslo and Helsinki games was a measly two.

We hope as you delve into this book it will rekindle childhood memories. Toys you may have played with, music your parents may have listened to and films you were taken to the cinema to see. We also hope that we bring you one or two surprising facts about the remarkable year you were born.

The Daily Headlines

No: 4583

THREE HALFPENCE

First Edition

Wednesday, February 6, 1952

King George VI
1895 - 1952

THE NATION MOURNS WITH THE NEWS THAT THE KING HAS DIED PEACEFULLY IN HIS SLEEP

The Daily Headlines

THREE HALFPENCE

Monday, July 28, 1952

No: 4687

First Edition

EMIL ZATOPEK WINS THREE GOLD MEDALS AT THE SUMMER OLYMPIC GAMES IN HELSINKI

The Daily Headlines

THREE HALFPENCE

Saturday, August 16, 1952

No: 4774

First Edition

TRAGEDY AS 34 LOSE THEIR LIVES IN CATASTROPHIC FLOODING IN LYNMOUTH

The Daily Headlines

No: 4851

THREE HALFPENCE

First Edition

Saturday, November 1, 1952

THE UNITED STATES SUCCESSFULLY DETONATES THE WORLD'S FIRST HYDROGEN BOMB

January	Medical student Ernesto "Che" Guevara and his biochemist friend embark on a motorcycle tour of South America. What they see shocks them as many people live in absolute poverty. They keep a diary of their trip and the journey not only has a profound impact on the two young men but also shapes South American politics for decades to come.
Jan 5th	Prime Minister Winston Churchill flies to Washington for an official state visit. Here he meets President Harry S. Truman, who is in the last year of his presidency. Topics of discussion are the special relationship, the atomic bomb and the Cold War – the battle between the capitalist West and the communist East.
Jan 10th	An Aer Lingus flight from London to Dublin crashes in the mountains of Snowdonia, North Wales, killing twenty passengers and three crew.
Jan 16th	Perennial favourite magician-dog-puppet, Sooty, makes his screen debut aided by the guiding hand of Harry Corbett.
Jan 26th	The Five-anti Campaign is launched in China. Its aim is to rid Communist China of corruption and Western bourgeois elements. It mirrors the Anti-communist McCarthyite witch hunts in America.
Jan 27th	The Chinese New Year starts. Those born between today and February 14th 1953 are born in the Year of the Dragon. They are outstandingly strong and attractive. Those born before January 27th were in the Year of the Cat and are affable and comfortable in any situation.
Feb 1st	The first television detector van comes into service. Around 150,000 Britons are estimated to be evading paying the licence fee.
Feb 6th	King George VI dies at home in Sandringham, Norfolk. His daughter Elizabeth is informed of the sad news whilst holidaying in the Treetops resort in Kenya.
Feb 6th	A mechanical heart is used for the first time on a human being. 41-year-old Henry Opitek is hooked up to the machine whilst undergoing heart bypass surgery at Wayne State University, Michigan.

Feb 7th　　Labour's Denis Healey becomes an MP by defeating the Conservative candidate with a three point swing at the Leeds South East by-election.

Feb 7th　　Elizabeth returns to England after a much delayed journey.

Feb 8th　　Elizabeth is proclaimed Queen Regnant (that is a Queen who rules outright with no King). The service takes place at St James's Palace. She is now Queen Elizabeth II of Great Britain and Northern Ireland and several Commonwealth countries.

Feb 10th　　The Congress Party of India, led by Pandit Jawaharlal Nehru, wins an outright victory in the country's first general election.

Feb 14th　　The Winter Olympics opens in Oslo, Norway. It lasts until 25th February. Great Britain are to win one gold medal when Jeanette Altwegg wins the figure skating.

Feb 15th　　The funeral of King George VI takes place at Windsor Castle. It is the first royal funeral to be televised live to the nation.

Feb 21st　　Prime Minister Winston Churchill declares "Freedom Day" as wartime identity cards are abolished.

Feb 26th　　Britain becomes the third nation after America and the Soviet Union to announce that they have a viable atomic bomb.

Mar 14th　　BBC Scotland is launched. The channel exclusively for viewers in Scotland opens with a performance by the Royal Scottish Country Dance Society.

Mar 15th / 16th　An incredible 73ins (185cm) of rain falls on Reunion Island in the Indian Ocean. This is more than three times the annual rainfall for London.

Mar 20th　　Stars gather to honour the best films of 1951 at The Oscars ceremony at the RKO Pantages Theatre. Humphrey Bogart takes the Best Actor Award for *The African Queen*. Vivien Leigh scoops the Best Actress Award and Karl Malden and Kim Hunter win the Best Supporting Oscars all for *A Streetcar Named Desire*. Surprisingly, the Best Picture Oscar goes to the musical *An American in Paris*, which won none of the other major awards.

Mar 21ˢᵗ   The Moondog Coronation Ball takes place in Cleveland Ohio. Not only is this event declared the first rock and roll concert, it also features both black and white performers. It is seen as a significant event in the Civil Rights Movement. Paul Williams, Tiny Grimes and Varetta Dillard entertain the 10,000 official ticket holders whose numbers are swelled by thousands of gate-crashers.

Mar 29ᵗʰ   The 98ᵗʰ Boat Race between Oxford and Cambridge takes place on the River Thames. In one of the closest finishes ever, Oxford win in a time of 20 minutes 23 seconds. On board the Cambridge boat is Adrian Cadbury, heir to the Cadbury empire.

Apr 6ᵗʰ   The African National Congress launches a campaign of defiance against the Apartheid regime in South Africa.

Apr 14ᵗʰ   Shridhar Cillal from Pune, India stops cutting his nails. His thumbnail would grow to almost two metres long and the combined length of his nails on one hand grew to over nine metres.

Apr 28ᵗʰ   The Allied occupation of Japan formally ends with a peace treaty signed in San Francisco. It is the only country to gain independence from a foreign power this year.

Apr 29ᵗʰ   The ANZUS defence treaty between Australia, New Zealand and the USA comes into force, offering the Southern hemisphere nations protection from China and Russia.

Apr 30ᵗʰ   Anne Frank's diary is first published in English. It chronicles the story of an adolescent Jewish girl's life who is confined to an Amsterdam attic whilst hiding from the Nazis. The diary tells of her hopes and dreams but abruptly ends on August 1ˢᵗ 1944, when she is betrayed and sent to Bergen-Belsen concentration camp to meet her death.

May 1ˢᵗ   The "Toy of the Year", Mr Potato Head, goes into production in the USA. The set contains toy hands, feet, ears, two mouths, two pairs of eyes, glasses, a pipe and facial hair. Early sets did not contain plastic heads as the pieces were designed to fit onto real potatoes.

May 2nd — After many hours of test flights the British built Comet becomes the world's first commercial jet airliner. It travels from London to Johannesburg making 4 stops along the way. The age of air travel for all has dawned.

May 3rd — Newcastle United beats Arsenal in the FA Cup Final. A solitary goal from Chilean striker George Robledo helps them to lift the cup for a record fifth time.

May 7th — The concept of the integrated circuit, the basis of all modern computers, is published by Yorkshireman Geoffrey W.A. Dummer. He presents his findings to a conference in Washington DC.

May 10th — The annual Cannes Film Festival draws to a close. The Grand Prix (Grand Prize) goes to Orson Welles for *Othello* and Renato Castellani for *Two Cents Worth of Hope*.

May 18th — Singer, actor, athlete, scholar, and political activist Paul Robeson performs an outdoor concert for more than 40,000 people gathered on both sides of the United States-Canadian border at Peace Arch Park in Blaine.

May 21st — A post office van is robbed in Eastcastle Street, London. The gang get away with over a quarter of a million pounds.

May 21st — The celebrated Hollywood actor John Garfield, 39, dies. He had been called before the House Committee on un-American activities. He had refused to name names and had been blacklisted by the Studios. He had been suffering from heart problems and stress.

May 27th — Elizabeth II makes her first visit as Queen to her Scottish home Balmoral. Crowds gather to greet her.

Jun 1st — The pledge of "free health care for all" is broken when a 5 shilling prescription fee is introduced. There are however some exemptions.

Jun 12th — In Bonham, Texas Dusty the cat gives birth to a single kitten. She enters the Guinness Book of records, not for this deed, but for this and the previous 419 kittens she bore.

Jun 13th   Irishman Reg Armstrong triumphs in the Isle of Man TT Race. He skilfully negotiates the treacherous Snaefell Mountain course aboard his Norton motorcycle.

Jun 15th   The Le Mans 24-hr race at Circuit de la Sarthe in Le Mans, France, comes to a close. The race signals the return of Mercedes-Benz to international motor racing, as the German team score a one-two finish with the W194 300 SL racing car that was specially developed for the 1952 racing season.

Jun 23rd   The touring Indian cricket team are greeted by the Queen at Lord's.

Jun 24th   KFC, Kentucky Fried Chicken, launch their first franchise in Salt Lake City, Utah. Soon the townsfolk are licking their fingers and proclaiming the secret recipe to be good.

Jul 5th   The London tram network, which had been running since the 1860s is taken out of service. Thousands take to the streets in the hope of having one last ride and to bid farewell to an icon of London life.

Jul 5th   The Wimbledon Lawn Tennis tournament ends. Maureen Connolly beats Louise Brough 7-5, 6-3 in the Ladies Singles. Frank Sedgman comes from behind to beat Jaroslav Drobny 4-6, 6-2, 6-3, 6-2. Sedgman also wins the doubles and mixed doubles making it a rare clean sweep of trophies.

Jul 11th   South African Bobby Locke comes from behind to win the Open Golf Championship at Royal Lytham St Annes.

Jul 13th   The Eighth Annual Cheltenham Festival of British Contemporary Music opens. The audience are treated to performances by the Halle Orchestra and the New London Quartet.

Jul 19th   The opening ceremony of the Helsinki Summer Olympics takes place. The games will run until August 3rd. Britain takes 1 gold, 2 Silver and 8 Bronze.

Jul 19th   Len Hutton is appointed England cricket captain. He holds the record for the highest single innings score in test cricket with his 364 against Australia at the Oval in 1938.

Jul 19th   The Tour de France cycle race ends with Italian rider Fausto Coppi entering the traditional finishing straight at the Champs-Élysées with an incredible half an hour lead.

Jul 23rd   France, West Germany, Italy, Belgium, Luxembourg and the Netherlands form the European Coal and Steel Community, an organisation that will develop into the European Union.

Jul 23rd   Revolution in Egypt sees the toppling of the monarch, King Farouk, and the rise to power of General Gamal Abdel Nasser.

Jul 26th   The annual Promenade Concerts "The Proms", open at the RoyalbAlbert Hall in West London. The first night starts with a resounding *God Save the Queen*. It is the first time the anthem dedicated to a female monarch has been heard at the Proms. The audience is then treated to works by Delius, Tchaikovsky and Wagner.

Jul 26th   Eva Peron "Evita", co-ruler of Argentina, dies aged 33.

Jul 31st   The swashbuckling epic *Ivanhoe*, starring Elizabeth Taylor and Robert Taylor, premieres in America. Under instruction from the House un-American Activities Committee, MGM remove the screenwriter Marguerite Roberts' name from the credits.

Aug 7th   The Chairing of the Bard ceremony at the Royal National Eisteddfod of Wales, in Aberystwyth, is televised by the BBC.

Aug 9th   The Korean war rages on and the Battle of Bunker Hill begins. United Nations Command, led by John T. Selden, struggle to hold off the Chinese People's Volunteer Army.

Aug 16th   34 people lose their lives and scores are injured when the village of Lynmouth in Devon is hit by severe flooding.

Aug 21st   The day sees the last confirmed sighting of a Caribbean Monk Seal off the coast of Colombia. It is later declared extinct.

Aug 29th   John Cage first "performs" his 4'33" piece. This involves four minutes and thirty-three seconds of silence. It was composed for any instrument, but with the instruction not to play them. Some get it, others don't.

Sep 4th   The Queen and The Duke of Edinburgh visit the Braemar Gathering in the Scottish Highlands. They are treated to traditional bagpipe music, sports and men dancing the Highland Fling.

Sep 6th   A DH 100 aeroplane breaks up in mid-air over the Farnborough Air Show. Tragically, 31 people are killed whilst crowds look on in horror.

Sep 17th   The Egremont Crab Fair is held for the fifth time in the Lake District. Its highlight is the gurning championships. Competitors remove their false teeth and then contort their faces to make them as small and as hideous as possible. This year the dubious honour of first prize goes to Mr. C. Walker.

Sep 19th   Whilst sailing to England for the premiere of his film Limelight, movie legend Charlie Chaplin is informed that he will be refused re-entry to the USA until he has been interrogated by the US Immigration Service. He sees the move as politically motivated and decides to remain in Europe.

Sep 20th   It is the Last Night of the Proms. The Prom-goers feast on Debussy, Britten, Liszt and Stravinsky, before singing along to Elgar's Pomp and Circumstance March No:1 in D Minor – *Land of Hope and Glory*.

Sep 23rd   In America, Vice-Presidential candidate Richard Nixon addresses the nation who are concerned about the use of funds in his campaign. This speech becomes known as the Checkers Speech, as Nixon announces that one gift he will not return is a dog called Checkers, who was a present for his children. "Tricky Dicky" seems to have got away with it this time.

Sep 26th   The body of 85-year-old May Helen Stacey is found in a top floor flat in London. Pathologists determine that she has probably been dead for six months. Her 62-year-old son, who had been drawing her pension, is charged with fraud. An open verdict was returned at her inquest. The coroner described it as 'a most extraordinary case in which a man had been living in two rooms with his mother's corpse for months'.

Sep 29th   The Manchester Guardian, in a break with tradition, prints news rather than advertisements on its front page for the first time.

Sep 29th   Whilst travelling at a speed in excess of 200 mph (320 km/h), John Cobb is killed as he attempts to break the world water speed record at Loch Ness in his boat, Crusader. During the run the boat hit an unexpected wake in the water and disintegrated around him. He was 52 years old.

Sep 30th   The battle of Bunker Hill draws to a conclusion. United Nations forces have held the strategically important hill. They lose around 100 men. Chinese forces also suffer heavy losses.

October   To coincide with the month of the birth of the inventor of dynamite, Alfred Nobel, prizes are handed out to people believed to be outstanding in their fields of expertise.

At the Nobel Peace Prize is awarded to Albert Schweitzer for "his altruism, reverence and tireless humanitarian work." The prize in Physiology and Medicine goes to Selman Waksman for his discovery of streptomycin, the first antibiotic effective against tuberculosis. The prize in Literature goes to François Mauriac "for his deep spiritual insight and the artistic intensity of his novels." This meets with the disapproval of the Pope who immediately condemns the award.

Oct 3rd   In an operation codenamed "Hurricane", Britain explodes its first atomic bomb in the Monte Bello Islands in Australia. The fallout contaminates a large area.

Oct 5th   After thirteen years, tea rationing ends and the good old British cuppa can be enjoyed freely once more.

Oct 8th   Three trains collide at Harrow and Wealdstone Station, North London. Driver, crew, passengers and people on the platform are among the 108 dead. It is the worst peacetime railway disaster in British history.

Oct 9th   The modernist 39-storey United Nations Building in Manhattan, New York, finally opens. It has been much delayed by a steelworkers' strike.

Oct 19th   Dr. Alain Bombard begins a solo journey across the Atlantic Ocean in a small Zodiac inflatable fitted with a sail. He takes no provisions with him. The object of the journey is to demonstrate that survival at sea is possible if you use certain techniques to catch food and harvest drinking water.

Oct 21st   Leading African nationalist Jomo Kenyatta is arrested following the declaration of a state of emergency in the British colony of Kenya.

Nov 1st   The United States successfully detonate "Mike", the world's first hydrogen bomb, on the Eniwetok Atoll in the Pacific Marshall Islands. The 10.4-megaton thermonuclear device, built upon the Teller-Ulam principles of staged radiation implosion, instantly vaporizes an entire island and leaves behind a crater more than a mile wide.

Nov 4th   Republican candidate Dwight D. Eisenhower wins a landslide victory in the US Presidential Election, thus ending a string of Democratic victories that stretch back to 1932. The Republicans also secure control of both Houses of Congress. Far left candidates secure 0.2% of the vote, but this fails to halt anti-communist paranoia.

Nov 4th   The Kamchatka Tsunami is generated by a magnitude 9.0 earthquake in Russia's far east. It generates waves as high as 50 feet and causes extensive damage to the Kamchatka Peninsula and the Kuril Islands. It leaves an estimated 10,000 to 15,000 people dead. In the Pacific, the largest damage occurs on the Hawaiian Islands with waves travelling as far as Peru, Chile and New Zealand. In Alaska, the Aleutian Islands and in California, waves of up to five feet are observed.

Nov 14th   The first UK music charts are published by the New Musical Express magazine. The first number one is Al Martino's *Here in My Heart*.

Nov 16th   Greece, the "birthplace of democracy," finally becomes one as women are accorded the right to vote for the first time.

Nov 18th   Albert Einstein is asked to stand for the Presidency of Israel. He declines stating "I know a little about nature and hardly anything about men."

Nov 25th   *The Mousetrap* by Agatha Christie makes its West End debut at the New Ambassadors Theatre, London.

Nov 29th   The first pillar box in Scotland bearing the insignia of Elizabeth II is vandalised. Many feel that is should read simply Queen Elizabeth, as England's Queen Elizabeth I (1533-1603) ruled before the 1707 Act of Union with Scotland.

Dec 4th   A great smog descends on London and much of Southeast England. It takes four days to lift and leaves thousands dead and many more with long-term breathing problems.

Dec 18th   Bill and Ben, The Flower Pot Men, make their screen debut accompanied by Little Weed.

Dec 20th   The Convention on the Political Rights of Women is approved by the UN. It seeks to extend female suffrage to all nations of the world.

Dec 23rd   Solo sailor Dr. Alain Bombard reaches Barbados having demonstrated that it is possible, with the correct survival skills, to survive at sea without provisions. His journey has taken him 65 days.

Dec 25th   Queen Elizabeth II delivers her first Christmas message. She announces that "Since my accession ten months ago, your loyalty and affection have been an immense support and encouragement. I want to take this Christmas Day, my first opportunity, to thank you with all my heart." And finishes with a plea to her subjects "At my Coronation next June, I shall dedicate myself anew to your service. I shall do so in the presence of a great congregation, drawn from every part of the Commonwealth and Empire, while millions outside Westminster Abbey will hear the promises and the prayers being offered up within its walls, and see much of the ancient ceremony in which Kings and Queens before me have taken part through century upon century. You will be keeping it as a holiday; but I want to ask you all, whatever your religion may be, to pray for me on that day- to pray that God may give me wisdom and strength to carry out the solemn promises I shall be making, and that I may faithfully serve Him and you, all the days of my life. May God bless and guide you all through the coming year."

 ### Sir Isaac Vivian Alexander Richards KNH OBE
born on 7th March 1952 in St. John's, Antigua and Barbuda

Viv Richards was the greatest batsman of his generation. He came into the game when fast bowling was at its most fearsome yet he was able to make the fast bowlers afraid of him. He came to the crease with a unique swagger, chewing gum and wielding his bat like a weapon. Unlike most players of his era Richards did not wear a helmet. In a series against Australia he was hit on the head by a bouncer bowled by Rodney Hogg. Richards simply shook his head and fixed his gaze on the bowler. The next ball, also a bouncer, was hooked into the crowd for six. He excelled at Test cricket as well as in the shorter 50 overs game. His highest test score was 291 at the Oval in 1976, but probably his best innings was his 189 at Old Trafford in a 50 overs game. With only the number 11 batsman Michael Holding for company, Richards hit shots to all sides of the ground leading the West Indies to victory. After the retirement of Clive Lloyd, Richards assumed the captaincy of the West Indies and led them to more glory. He is one of the few captains in test history never to have lost a series.

In 2000 Richards was named as one of the Top 5 cricketers of the century by the Wisden Cricketers' Almanack alongside Sir Donald Bradman, Sir Garfield Sobers, Sir Jack Hobbs and Shane Warne. His great rivalry with England's Sir Ian Botham was only on the pitch as the two became great friends with Richards becoming godfather to Botham's son, Liam.

 ### Douglas Noel Adams
born on 11th March 1952 in Cambridge, England

Douglas Adams always claimed that he was ill-prepared for the worldwide success of his most famous undertaking, *The Hitch Hiker's Guide to the Galaxy*. He described the adulation as "like being helicoptered to the top of Mount Everest." The Guide started off as a radio programme in 1978 then moved to television and the stage as well as spawning four books, selling fifteen million copies.

Hollywood bought the rights to make a film but it spent over two decades stuck in the system. Adams, always one to find the right words, likened the process to "trying to grill a steak by having a succession of people coming into the room and breathing on it." Adams died aged 49 in 2001 and would not see the film version of his work which was released in 2005. The success of his magnum opus allowed Adams to indulge in his hobbies and obsessions; he acquired a large collection of electric guitars and worked to protect endangered species.

Whilst studying at Cambridge Adams decided to hitchhike across Europe to Istanbul. This experience sparked the idea that someone could hitchhike across the Universe.

 ## Dermot John Morgan
born on 31st March 1952 in Dublin, Ireland

Morgan gained entry to University College Dublin where he studied English and Philosophy. In 1974 he took up a teaching post but left two years later to pursue the comedy career that he had started at university. In 1979 his introduction to TV came with an appearance on *Live Mike* on RTE television as Father Trendy, a hip catholic priest. He became a regular for the next four years and this religious, yet irreligious, role won him a cult following.

His career took a slump in the mid-eighties, when his humour didn't fit in with the conservative views of the state broadcaster. In 1988 he set up his own production company, Cue Productions, and began work on a radio show called *Scrap Saturday*. This show lampooned Irish politicians, and allowed him to use his brilliant talent for mimicry. In 1991, at the height of its success the show was cancelled, much to Morgan's annoyance. In 1995 he began starring in his most popular show, *Father Ted* for which he is best remembered.

Ted Fest is an annual event held on the Isle of Inishmore off the coast of County Galway in Ireland. Attendees dress up and recreate scenes from the series.

 ## Jean Paul Gaultier MBE
born on 24th April 1952 in Arcueil, France

The story of how Gaultier rose from obscurity to become the enfant terrible of the fashion world is remarkable. As a child he enjoyed spending time with his grandmother who encouraged his artistic talents. At the age of 15 he became obsessed with the film *Falbalas* which is regarded as one of the finest movies about the world of haute couture. This encouraged Jean Paul to create his own designs and send them to the leading French fashion houses of the day. His sketches caught the eye of Pierre Cardin who offered Gaultier a job on his 18th birthday. After a year he left to work alongside Jacques Esterel before joining Jean Patou's team in 1971.

However three years later he returned to the team that launched him. Pierre Cardin commissioned the young and ambitious Gaultier to design a collection aimed at the American market. In 1976 he established his own fashion label where he drew inspiration from the punk scene and challenged gender stereotypes. It is for his collaborations with Madonna that Gaultier is most famous, particularly that iconic conical bra.

Not only has Gaultier won awards for costume design in the film industry, most notably for *The Fifth Element*, he is not shy in front of the camera and has made cameo appearances on screen. His ability to ham it up was best seen in the series *Absolutely Fabulous*.

William John "Liam" Neeson OBE
born on 7th June 1952 in Ballymena, Northern Ireland

Neeson's path into acting was a most unorthodox one. He was a champion boxer, where he gained his characterful crooked nose, a part-time footballer and a fork-lift truck driver in a Guinness factory. He then trained as a teacher before joining the Lyric Players' Theatre in Belfast. He finished his acting apprenticeship at Ireland's National Theatre, The Abbey in Dublin. In 1980 filmmaker John Boorman saw him on stage in Steinbeck's *Of Mice and Men* and offered him the part of Sir Gawain in *Excalibur*. It was Neeson's big break.

A host of supporting roles followed and he was able to act alongside the likes of Julie Andrews and Julia Roberts. Neeson finally got his name at the top of the bill when he landed the role of the industrialist who saved thousands of Jews from Nazi extermination in *Schindler's List*. He then cemented his position as a Hollywood A-lister with roles in the *Star Wars* franchise before, fittingly for an Irish Catholic, playing a priest in Scorsese's *Gangs of New York*.

Late on in his career Neeson has built a reputation for tough-guy, action hero roles, most notably in the *Taken* trilogy. Neeson expected the first film in the series to flop but took the role as it gave him the opportunity to spend four months in Paris whilst learning karate.

Celia Diana Savile Imrie
born on 15th July 1952 in Guildford, Surrey, England

Celia Imrie is one of Britain's best loved actresses. As well as her acclaimed film, television and theatre work, she is also a Sunday Times best-selling author. She is the most adaptable of thespians, equally at home in either serious or comedic roles. Much of her best known work came through her friendship with Victoria Wood. She appeared in the TV series *Dinner Ladies* as well as on stage in the hilarious *Acorn Antiques: The Musical*, for which she won an Olivier award. She is also much loved for her film roles including *The Best Exotic Marigold Hotel*, *Bridget Jones's Diary*, *Calendar Girls* and *Mamma Mia! Here We Go Again*.

She has an extensive list of theatre credits, having appeared in *Pygmalion*, *Henry V*, *Macbeth* and alongside Dame Judi Dench in a universally acclaimed production of *King Lear* in 2016. Her debut novel, *Not Quite Nice*, was described in The Times as being a "delicious piece of entertainment" and it spent six weeks in the top ten bestseller list.

When Imrie was a guest on the BBC genealogy programme *Who Do You Think You Are?* she found out that she was related to William, Lord Russell who was executed for treason in 1683.

Alexei David Sayle
born on 7th August 1952 in Anfield, Liverpool, England

The comedian and writer Alexei Sayle launched his stand-up career in 1979 in the fledgling itinerant Comedy Store often sharing venues with seedy strip clubs. He appeared alongside future stars such as Dawn French, Jennifer Saunders and Tony Allen. His tight fitting suits and abrasive character soon made him a household name. Sell-out tours followed as did TV appearances such as the landlord in *The Young Ones*. A novelty single *Ullo John! Got a New Motor?* further propelled him into the public consciousness.

Later he stepped back from performing and published novels and short stories, many of which are semi-autobiographical, like *Stalin Ate My Homework*, which alludes to the fact he was raised in a communist household. The spoken word was always his forte and he returned to stand-up and created a number of comedy series for BBC radio, including Alexei Sayle's *Imaginary Sandwich Bar*.

"People are more violently opposed to fur than leather because it's safer to harass rich women than motorcycle gangs." A. Sayle.

John Graham Mellor aka "Joe Strummer"
born on 21st August 1952 in Ankara, Turkey

Joe Strummer formed The Clash in 1976 and along with the Sex Pistols they spearheaded the British punk scene. By 1979 The Clash had broadened their musical repertoire at a time when most punk bands were stagnating. Under Strummer's direction they incorporated reggae, ska and rockabilly into their work. By the 1980s the band were playing to packed audiences around the world. Strummer found reconciling his punk ethics and new found fame difficult and tensions within the band led to a split.

Although Strummer continued with new members, his interest in music began to wane. It is then that he turned to acting. His first role was as a grimy gangster in the cult classic *Straight to Hell Returns* where Strummer employed the method school of acting and did not change his clothes during the filming. After a ten year hiatus Strummer returned to music with the excellent album *Rock Art and the X-ray Style*. Just before The Clash were due to be inducted into the Rock and Roll Hall of Fame, Strummer died, aged just 50.

A pedestrian underpass at the junction of Edgware Road and Harrow Road, West London, was renamed the Joe Strummer Subway in 2009 as Strummer used to busk there.

James Scott "Jimmy" Connors

born on 2nd September 1952 in Belleville, Illinois, USA

Connors was one of America's greatest tennis players. When he took up the game he did not know what fame and fortune would follow. Alongside John McEnroe he was one half of a pairing that formed America's golden era of tennis. He was known, for good reason, as the "Heavyweight Champion" as his approach to the game was confrontational and gladiatorial. Connors was a snarling, fist-pumping all-action type of player. In McEnroe he met a worthy adversary and their battles always brought massive viewing figures. Jimbo's attitude to the game is best summed up in his own words when he said "I hate to lose more than I like to win, I hate to see the happiness on their faces when they beat me."

Throughout a long and fruitful career Connors garnered 109 singles titles, including 8 majors and spent 268 weeks as world No.1. Outside of his battles with McEnroe it is his loss to Arthur Ashe at Wimbledon in 1975 for which he is best remembered. Ashe's strategy was to return the ball softly causing the combative Connors to punch himself out.

Connors' career spanned an incredible 19 years, earning him the title "The Comeback King". He won 107 singles matches at Wimbledon between 1972 and 1991.

Nile Gregory Rodgers Jr.

born on 19th September 1952 in New York City, USA

The career of Nile Rodgers is one of the most prolific and enduring in popular music history. He started playing guitar whilst still at school and there was no stopping this emerging talent. By the age of 19 he was not only performing regularly on the children's TV show *Sesame Street*, he was also part of the house band at the world famous Apollo Theatre in Harlem. There he played with the greats such as Aretha Franklin and Ben E. King. Rodgers then strove to form a band of his own and found a perfect partner in Bernard Edwards and together they formed CHIC.

Hit after hit followed as they introduced an unmistakable dance rhythm into the world. Soon the New York disco goers were moving to the hits *Dance, Dance, Dance, Everybody Dance* and *Le Freak*. Rodgers had caught the attention of other musicians who lined up to collaborate with him. Work with such diverse talents as David Bowie, Madonna, Eric Clapton, Duran Duran and INXS followed. In 1996 he was selected by his peers as Billboard Magazine's Top Producer in the World.

Rodgers says his greatest regret is not collaborating with Miles Davis when the jazz great asked him to do so. He thought Davis was joking.

 ## Christopher D'Olier Reeve
born on 25th September 1952 in New York City, USA

Reeve was a bright child. After graduating from high school he gained entry into the Ivy league university, Cornell. There he combined his studies with pursuing a career as a professional actor. In his final year he was one of two students selected to study at New York's world famous performing arts conservatory, the Juilliard School. The other student selected was Robin Williams and the two formed a life-long friendship. In 1978 Reeve landed the role of Superman. His physique – he was 6ft 4ins – and chiselled good looks made him perfect for the part. However, getting the role was a double-edged sword.

While it was difficult for people to imagine any other actor as Superman, it was equally hard for them to see Reeve playing any other character. He was to play the superhero four times on the big screen. One other role he did play was filled with a tragic irony. In the film *Above Suspicion* Reeve played a paralysed police officer. Six days after its release in 1995, Reeve broke his neck in a riding accident which left him paralysed for the rest of his life.

A commercial during the Super Bowl in 2000 portrayed Reeve as being able to walk, via computer animation. The next day the medical company featured in the commercial was flooded with calls asking how they cured him. Sadly they hadn't.

Imran Ahmed Khan Niazi HI PP
born on 5th October 1952 in Lahore, Pakistan

In cricket and in life Imran Khan is a true all rounder. He graduated from Oxford University where he captained the cricket team. This led him into the Pakistan national team where he again rose to be captain. The pinnacle of his cricketing career was leading his side to victory in the 1992 World Cup. He is considered one of the greatest all-rounders in cricket history, averaging 38 with the bat and 22 with the ball. Deeply affected by the death of his mother, he founded a cancer hospital in Lahore in 1994 and it became Pakistan's state-of-the-art facility for its poorest citizens.

His philanthropy then extended to education when he established Namal College in the rural district of Mainwali. This engagement with the poor and dispossessed made him popular with the people. Khan always had one eye on politics and after several unsuccessful attempts, in 2018 he rose to become the 22nd Prime Minister of Pakistan.

When Richie Benaud picked his greatest ever World XI team in 2004 he named Imran Khan as captain.

Sharon Rachel Osbourne
born on 9th October 1952 in Brixton, London, England

Sharon's father, Don Arden, was a music agent, managing the careers of artists including Jerry Lee Lewis, Little Richard, ELO and, most significantly, Black Sabbath. During her childhood she was surrounded by musical legends. When she was 15 she started working for her father's company where, a couple of years later, she met John Michael Osbourne, the Black Sabbath singer, who went by the name Ozzy. In 1979 Ozzy left Black Sabbath and was sacked by Arden. It was then that Sharon decided to be his manager, a decision that caused an irreconcilable rift with her father. Within three years Ozzy and Sharon were married. The marriage was often troubled but Sharon bore three children: Aimee, Kelly and Jack.

In 2001 MTV ran a groundbreaking series called *The Osbournes* which proved a huge ratings hit. The series showed the family, warts and all, in their Los Angeles home. It made stars of their children Kelly and Jack, but Aimee would have nothing to do with it. Sharon went on to be a judge on *The X Factor* and has also hosted a talk show of her own.

Sharon's husband, Ozzy, was arrested and banned from playing in the city of San Antonio after he was caught urinating on the Alamo Cenotaph in a drunken state wearing one of her dresses.

Jennifer Ann Agutter OBE
born on 20th December 1952 in Taunton, Somerset, England

Jenny Agutter was born in Somerset. Her father was a British army officer so she had an itinerant childhood, living in many different countries, including Singapore, Germany and Cyprus. When in England, she trained at Elmhurst Ballet School and, at just aged seven, was cast in Walt Disney's film *Ballerina*. Numerous film and television parts followed, culminating in her breakthrough role as Roberta in the BBC serialisation of E. Nesbit's *The Railway Children*. She then travelled the globe in search of work, eventually filming the haunting drama *Walkabout* in Australia.

Her career seemed to stall before Lionel Jeffries asked her to reprise her role in a film version of *The Railway Children*. After this, offers of work started to pour in; her role of Fritha in *The Snow Goose* won her an Emmy Award. This raised her profile in America and after a season at the National Theatre in London, she headed to Hollywood. Jenny was given a leading role in the sci-fi drama *Logan's Run* alongside fellow Brit, Michael York. Other film roles included, *An American Werewolf in London* and *Equus*, before she lit up our small screens in *Call the Midwife*.

Agutter works tirelessly for several charities. One, The Cystic Fibrosis (CF) Trust, is particularly close to her heart. Like 1 in 25 of the UK population she is a carrier of the CF gene.

Hunt Emerson
born on 28th January 1952 in Birmingham, England

Emerson was closely involved with the Birmingham Arts Lab of the late 1970s, before immersing himself in the British Underground comic scene in the 1980s. Children will be familiar with his work in the Beano comic, but Hunt has covered all facets of human nature with works about politics, poetry, history and sex. His interpretations of literature stand out, most notably his *Rime of the Ancient Mariner*, *Dante's Inferno* and the raunchy *Casanova's Last Stand*. His illustrations can be seen in The Radio Times, Time Out and Melody Maker amongst others.

Clive Stuart Anderson
born on 10th December 1952 in Middlesex, England

Anderson first trained as a barrister before leaving that career to concentrate on comedy. He was the first act to appear at London's Comedy Store when it opened in 1979. He later appeared at the Edinburgh Fringe with Griff Rhys Jones and won a British Comedy Award. His aloof acerbic style stood him in good stead when he presented the TV improvisation show *Whose Line is it Anyway* for ten series, but it also got him into trouble. The Bee Gees famously walked out during their interview on his chat show, *Clive Anderson All Talk*.

Other Notable Births

Ryuichi Sakamoto
17th January 1952
Composer | Pianist

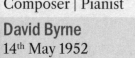
Joey Dunlop
25th February 1952
Motorcycle Racer

Bill Beaumont
9th March 1952
Rugby Player

David Byrne
14th May 1952
Singer | Songwriter

Isabella Rossellini
18th June 1952
Actor | Author

John Goodman
20th June 1952
Actor

Dan Aykroyd
1st July 1952
Actor | Comedian

Stewart Copeland
16th July 1952
Musician | Composer

David Hasselhoff
17th July 1952
Actor | Singer

Louis Walsh
5th August 1952
TV Judge | Manager

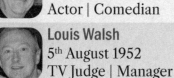
Nelson Piquet
17th August 1952
Racing Driver

Patrick Swayze
18th September 1952
Actor | Singer

Clive Barker
5th October 1952
Author

Jeff Goldblum
22nd October 1952
Actor | Musician

Roseanne Barr
3rd November 1952
Actor | Comedian

👑 King George VI
died aged 56 on 6th February 1952 at Sandringham House, England

Alfred Fredrick Arthur George, known simply as "Bertie" to his family, was a man born not to be king. As the second son of George V he expected to live a quiet life. When his older brother Edward's scandalous relationship with American divorcee Wallis Simpson led to his abdication, the crown passed to George. At first it was not worn easily, he was shy and suffered from a stutter, which made him seem distant to his people. Speech therapy slowly helped him overcome his impediment. It was the war that would come to define George. The King was advised to leave London but he steadfastly refused to go in spite of Buckingham Palace suffering two direct hits. With his wife Queen Elizabeth (later the Queen Mother), he toured the country visiting bomb sites and army bases, boosting morale. This more than anything won over his subjects. The death of George, the man who had greatness thrust upon him, was greeted with a genuine outpouring of grief.

🗣 Richard Stafford Cripps
died aged 62 on 21st April 1952 in Zurich, Switzerland

Cripps was a chemist, a barrister, a diplomat and subsequently a politician. He was described as a man who believed firmly and did faithfully. It is through the lasting effect he had on British politics that he can best be judged. In 1947 he became the first person to combine the offices of Minister of Economic Affairs and the Chancellor of the Exchequer. He stressed with conviction the need for improved productivity and restraint in expenditure. This he argued would provide fairness for all and help pay for the proposed National Health Service. That he was largely able to bring both trade unions and business on board was testament to his powers as a politician. Historian Kenneth O. Morgan wrote that Cripps was "the real architect of the rapidly improving economic picture." A decade later a Conservative Prime Minister, Harold Macmillan, would be able to proclaim "You've never had it so good."

🩺 Maria Tecla Artemisia Montessori
died aged 81 on 6th May 1952 in Noordwijk, Netherlands

Montessori was born into a well-to-do, well-connected family. As a young woman she pursued a career in medicine. After she qualified, she specialised in psychiatry and child development, but she found the male dominated profession stifling. It was then she turned to education. Her philosophy was the belief that children should be allowed to develop at their own pace. She laid out the principles in a book *The Montessori Method*. It became highly influential, with many educators following her methods. Broadly speaking children under 6 were encouraged to explore their immediate environment whilst those 6-12 were directed towards abstract concepts and the use of their imagination. There are now around 20,000 Montessori schools worldwide. Those who benefitted from her methods include Prince William, Jeff Bezos, Jacqueline Kennedy and Sean "P.Diddy" Combs.

Wilfred Reid "Wop" May OBE DFC
died aged 56 on 21st June 1952 in Utah, USA

May as a young boy acquired the nickname "Wop" through a cousin who couldn't pronounce Wilfred. He applied to join the Royal Flying Corps in 1917. His first flight resulted in the destruction of his own and another plane. However, he was accepted into the RFC. On April 18th, 1918, May was involved in his first dogfight. Luckily the German Fokker aircraft crashed of its own accord. The next day, May took to the air again with strict instructions from his squadron leader to stay out of fights. However May could not resist. Soon his machine gun jammed and, worse still, Manfred Von Richthofen, "The Red Baron", was on his tail. The Red Baron left himself exposed and was shot down by RFC fighters. Showing typical Canadian modesty May later put his survival down to his novice fighting which was so erratic it confused Germany's greatest flying ace. May's flying prowess did improve. He was credited with downing around 20 enemy planes.

Maria Eva Duarte de Peron "Evita"
died aged 33 on 26th July 1952 in Buenos Aires, Argentina

Evita was a force of nature. Born in poverty, she rose to be the most powerful woman in the world. At 16 she left home to pursue an acting career. She got a job with a radio station where she met President Juan Peron whom she would later marry. Through her radio work she gained support for her husband, notably amongst women pushing him to electoral success. Their marriage was one based on equality, which was remarkable in the deeply conservative Argentina of the time. Evita chaired the Peronist Women's Party, ran the Ministries of Labour and Health and set up a foundation to provide food and medicine for the poor. Her work led her to become the spiritual leader of Argentina. By 1951 her health began to decline. In an act of callous cruelty her husband persuaded doctors to hide her cancer diagnosis lest it affect upcoming elections, illustrating how pivotal to the President's success Evita had become. She died a year later.

Hattie McDaniel
died aged 59 on 26th October 1952 in Los Angeles, California, USA

Hattie, who was the child of parents born into slavery, was a singer-songwriter, comedienne and actress. She is best remembered for her role as Mammy the maid in *Gone with the Wind*. The film premiered in segregated Atlanta, Georgia where Hattie was barred from attending. Her fellow star, Clark Gable, wanted to boycott the event but Hattie talked him out of it. Hattie's role earned her a Best Supporting Actress Oscar - the first Academy Award given to a person of colour. Again segregation reared its ugly head at the ceremony where she had to sit separately from white people. She had four short marriages. Each husband was either jealous of her success or wished to exploit her wealth. She received criticism from sections of the African-American community who felt her film roles were demeaning. But Hattie did what she had to do and through her work in housing and civil rights she left the world a better place.

The Coins We Used

19 years before decimalisation, we used the system of **pounds**, **shillings** and **pence** commonly represented using the symbols **£sd**. The **£** symbol evolved over many years from the letter **L** which derives from the Latin word *libra*, meaning a pound of money. Although **s** is the first letter of the word shilling, the use of the letter derives from the Latin word *solidus* which means coin. The curious use of the letter **d** for pennies also has a Latin origin from the word *denarius* meaning containing ten. Unlike the decimal system based on multiples of 10, the pre-decimal system was based on multiples of 12. There were 12 pennies to a shilling and 240 pennies to a pound. This meant there were 20 shillings to the pound. In 1952 there were 9 coins in circulation with evocative names that still permeate our language today.

Farthing ¼ d

In use to 1961

With 4 farthings to a penny, these smallest of coins featured a smooth edge and a wren on the reverse. *He hasn't got two farthings to rub together* was a popular expression to describe someone poor.

Halfpenny ½ d

In use to 1969

Commonly known as the *ha'penny* it is was the only word in the English language with a silent 'f'. Since 1937 the coin featured Sir Francis Drake's ship The Golden Hind. The popular pub game *Shove Ha'penny* features 5 halfpennies.

Penny 1d

In use to 1971

Before 1860 the penny was a large copper coin. This is why bicycles with a large front wheel were nicknamed Penny Farthings. Popular expressions using the penny include *ten a penny* and *a penny for your thoughts*.

Threepence 3d

In use to 1971

These 12-sided coins were commonly known as *thruppence* or *thrupenny bits*. The silver versions known as *joeys* were often hidden in Christmas puddings making an exciting find for the lucky children who discovered them.

Sixpence 6d

In use to 1980

These silver coins reputedly brought good luck. Sixpences were placed in bride's shoes as a wedding gesture. Known as benders, they could easily be bent. *Going on a bender* derived from drinking all day in pubs with sixpence.

Shilling 1/-

In use to 1990

First minted in the reign of Henry VII as a testoon, the shilling was latterly commonly known as a bob. *Taking the king's shilling* meant enrolling in the army whilst *A few bob short of a pound* describes someone a bit dim.

Florin 2/-

In use to 1992

The florin was Britain's first decimal coin in response to calls in the mid 19th Century for decimal coinage to be introduced. As 2 *bob* the florin was worth 1/10th of a pound. After decimalisation in 1971 florins became worth 10 pence.

Half Crown 2/6

In use to 1969

Half crowns were originally struck in gold in the reign of Henry VIII. The first silver half crowns were issued under Edward VI in 1549. Surviving for over 450 years, the half crown was one of the most successful coins of all time.

Crown 5/-

In use to present day

The British crown is a heavy silver coin. Rarely spent, crowns are often minted for commemorative purposes. After decimalisation a crown was worth 25p until 1990 when their face value was changed to £5.

The average annual wage in the UK in 1952 was approximately:

£375-£450

The Morris Minor was introduced in the UK in 1948. Designed by Alec Issigonis who would later go on to design the Mini, this series II Morris Minor launched in 1952 would cost approximately:

£600 - £650

The price of the average house would be approximately 5-6x the average annual wage. Depending on where you were in the country this meant the price of a typical 1930's 3-bedroom semi-detached house would be in the region of:

£1,750 - £2,250

The Bush TV22 television set had an iconic Bakelite design holding a 9" screen receiving only one channel. Very expensive for the average family, they cost:

£35 12s

In 1952 the government raised the minimum cost of a small loaf of bread by ¾d to:

3¾d

A gallon of petrol (which is equivalent to 4.5 litres) cost:

4s 3d

National Service

National service recruits enjoying a cup of tea whilst off duty in a NAAFI

Indian and British soldiers in Korea

National Service was introduced in 1947 to overcome challenges and resolve military manpower shortages in the wake of World War II. Wartime conscription was extended into an obligatory period of National Service for men of military age. Over 2 million were called up to the armed forces, often serving in one of Britain's many colonial outposts around the world.

After passing a medical and joining up, all conscripts had six weeks of basic training during which they got used to military life. Once enlisted and inside camp National Servicemen were issued with their equipment, which often consisted of ill-fitting uniforms and boots. Conscripts were knocked into shape by sergeants under pressure to train them in as short a time as possible. Most conscripts lived in cold barracks with primitive toilets and washing facilities. The lucky few had newly built, brick barracks with central heating. Some were housed in a 'Barrack Spider' - a wooden hut with eight rooms and a central washing area. Up to twenty men were housed in each room. Each man had a steel wardrobe, an iron bed and a one-foot locker for small items of kit. Overseas accommodation varied a lot. Servicemen could find themselves sharing a tent with three other men, such as in camps in Cyprus, or even as many as 15, as in war-torn Korea.

The camps and accommodation for servicemen in the Suez Canal Zone were amongst the worst, but those in Germany were generally of a high standard. Recruits soon began the seemingly endless task of polishing kit and equipment. Many regarded this as mindless drill aimed at destroying individuality. However, this strict regime helped foster a group identity and brought recruits closer together with many lifelong friendships being formed. Officers who did four years or more on a Short Service Commission were allowed to train in a speciality. Many other ranks were trained in general clerical duties, such as typing. Some received more specific training in technical subjects, such as communications and engineering. Languages were also taught at the Joint Service School of Languages at Bodmin. Russian was especially useful in this Cold War era. For those stationed in war zones, the possibility of death was suddenly part of daily life. The experience many men had of being thrown into combat situations, such as in Korea, Malaysia and Egypt, would never be forgotten. Men with minimal training were expected to fight hardened guerrilla fighters or cope with riots or civil unrest. Between 1947 and 1963, a total of 395 National Servicemen were killed on active duty.

Office Life

The first thing that would strike you if you were transported back to a British office in 1952, is that there was very little plugged in to the wall. Virtually everything from typewriters to adding machines were manual. In large offices, the typing pool, which was almost universally staffed by women, was a noisy place. Correcting mistakes was done either by correction fluid or a ribbon, which necessitated the typist using a backspace key and retyping the offending letter or word thereby masking it. Often, letters would look a bit of a mess so accuracy was highly prized. Secretarial training was considered a good move for young women and gave them an income and financial freedom.

A state of the art office environment in 1952

An employee creating punch cards

For many it was a job to do before marriage and domestic life, and it was always a good skill to have as it gave them "something to fall back on". After marriage, work as a school secretary was sought after as it allowed married woman to continue working in the knowledge that their hours and holidays coincided with their children's. There were virtually no computers, in fact the term was more likely to describe a person than it was a machine. The photocopier, invented in the US, was still in development and was virtually no use at all. One copy would take up to fifteen minutes to produce, meaning that it was often quicker to have a secretary type the letter again. Larger offices were very regimented places. The managers, nearly all men, would have separate toilet facilities, dining rooms and in some places even lifts. The general staff, consisting of mainly female secretaries, maintenance men and messenger boys shared the general staff canteen, which was often a more fun place to be.

The glass ceiling for women, except in very rare cases, was reached when usually a more mature woman became a personal secretary to a manager. Along with all general clerical duties, she was charged with running the manager's schedule, organising and laying out meetings, attending to the diary, answering phone calls and especially on a Friday after many a manager had a liquid lunch, telling people that her boss was "currently indisposed." It would take decades for the British office to become more egalitarian places where staff were not employed on the basis of gender or the colours of an old school tie.

Secretaries hard at work in the typing pool

Life on the Farm

Farm machinery replaced work originally done by labourers

A family on their summer break helping with the harvest

Farming in Britain was in a state of great flux in 1952. A new age of mechanisation was dawning as the country emerged from the war years. Back then the call to "Dig for Victory" encouraged food production on every spare acre of land. Even in 1952, seven years after the end of the war, food shortages still prevailed with farming strictly controlled by the Government. The Journal of the Ministry of Agriculture announced that "The world food outlook is very grave indeed….a united effort on the part of scientists and farmers will be needed if the situation is to be saved". Farmers quickly noted that the ministry mentioned scientists first with this causing tension between those who worked the land and those who told them how to do it. Through subsidy and control the government encouraged the production of arable crops, milk, pork and eggs. This led to a marked increase in the price of other produce with food shortages still prevalent. Although mechanisation helped with the workload, most work was done by hand.

The life of a farm labourer was tough. Ploughing and harvesting were increasingly done by machine but such tasks as milking cows, digging drainage channels and bailing hay were done by hand. Farmers, as they do today, largely lived by the hours of daylight; harvest time in the Autumn was particularly arduous. In the summertime when fruit was at its most bountiful, families and teenage children travelled from the towns and cities to help with the harvest. A hangover from this persists to this day; it is the reason children are given six weeks' summer holiday. However, British kids should have been thankful that they did not grow up in Ireland where they had three months "holiday".

Famously, London schoolchildren were sent by coach to Kent to help with hop picking for the brewing industry. Many had fond memories of the experience, but most often living conditions were poor, pay was minimal and some yearned for the relative tranquillity of home and even school! For farmers, the highlight of the year, as it is today, was the country show. This was and is an age old celebration of all things rural. There were dances, food aplenty, tug of war contests between the rufty-tufty farmhands and the quaffing of large amounts of the local brew. These were also places where business was done and contests for the best livestock often resulted in the winner changing hands for a princely sum.

The Primary School

In 1952 there were no state funded nurseries. For most children their early life centred around the home, cared for by a stay-at-home mother or other members of their extended family. Children entered school at the age of five and for many it was a big shock. Many tears were shed at the school gates as mothers loosened their grip both literally and metaphorically. The day would start with assembly and a roll-call, the register. Children would sit cross-legged on the floor and listen to an address from the headteacher which was followed by the singing of a hymn. It was then on to the classroom.

A game of marbles in the playground

A lesson in how to hold the bat

Each pupil was assigned their own desk, this normally faced the front of the classroom. The desk had a flap with storage space underneath and an inkwell at its upper edge. Children were eased gently into school life and little was done on the first day. Upon returning home many were surprised to find out that they had to do it again the next day. When lessons became serious there was much emphasis on the "three Rs": reading, writing and arithmetic. This immediately confused many as only one of the subjects actually began with R. Reading often involved reciting poetry or prose from memory or reading passages of a book aloud. Writing was not only a test of spelling and grammar, but also of handwriting skills. Pupils normally wrote in pencil except when they were taught rudimentary calligraphy. Some fared better than others and the skills learned stayed with them through to adulthood.

For others it was torture as each pupil was at the mercy of the children who had used the nib pen before them. Each pen was worn down in different ways and this bias was particularly difficult for left-handers. Arithmetic (maths) involved learning the times table, usually up to the number 12. The Britain of the day was pre-decimal and had 12 pennies to a shilling so knowing how to count in twelves was useful. There were few gizmos, the teacher stood at the front of the class and wrote on a blackboard. The pupils would have little more than a geometry set consisting of a set square, a protractor, a metal compass, a pencil and sharpener and a stencil. Other than the pencil most items were rarely used.

There was also music and movement, and gym. Music and movement encouraged free expression, but most pupils of the day can only remember being asked to pretend that they were a tree swaying in the wind. Gym involved vaulting and climbing over a mini assault course. This was a hangover from military training during the war and was performed in underwear. Eleven was a crucial age for children as they had to sit the Eleven-plus exam. Very often it would shape the rest of their lives. If you passed you went to a grammar school, failure would see you go to a secondary modern or technical college.

Children at a primary school in Wales

Background

After the Second World War, the state funded secondary education system was divided using a Tripartite system containing grammar schools, secondary technical colleges and secondary modern schools. The Eleven-plus examination was used to select which pupils went to which schools based on ability. As technical colleges were not available on the scale envisaged the exam came to symbolise fierce competition for places at the prestigious grammar schools. The very name still deeply divides opinion with many believing it was the symbol of a segregated two-tier school system whilst for others it set the educational benchmark.

Here's your chance to test yourself with example questions from the 1950s:
(Answers on page 92)

Arithmetic Questions

Question One: A motorist who left home at 11.15am, drives at 36 miles per hour. He stops for lunch from 1.15pm to 2.45pm and then continues his journey at 40 miles per hour. How many miles in total has he travelled by 6pm?

Question Two: 785 is multiplied by 50 and the result is divided by 125. Write down the answer.

Question Three: A ship uses 200 gallons of diesel for a voyage of 300 miles. How far could it travel using 80 gallons?

Question Four: Write in figures the sum of three hundred and seventy six and eighty-nine.

Question Five: Elizabeth is 8 years old and her father is 38. Answer the following:

A) How old was Elizabeth's father when he was 6 times as old as her?

B) In how many years' time will her father be three times as old as Elizabeth?

C) How old will Elizabeth be when her father becomes 15 times as old as she was 4 years ago?

General Intelligence Questions

Question One: Each of the following jumbled sentences can make sense by interchanging two words. Rewrite the sentences:

A) A was stung by Billy bee.
B) The shepherd whistled by the gate and stood to his dog.
C) The swim went to the pool for a family.

Question Two: The letters PELAP are the letters of the word APPLE jumbled up. Rearrange the following:

A) TOUNOCC is a fruit which comes from abroad.
B) FARFIGE is a large animal.
C) TIPACRAI is a girl's name.

Question Three: Each of the following sentences contains one error. Rewrite the sentences correctly:

A) When the dog saw me, it wagged it's tail.
B) The subject doesn't concern you or I.
C) Whilst speaking to my brother, the police car past me.

Top 10 Girls' Baby Names [1]

1. Susan	of Hebrew origin meaning "Lily Rose"
2. Linda	from the German for *lime tree* via Spanish where it meant "Pretty"
3. Christine	of Latin and French origin meaning "Follower of Christ"
4. Margaret	from *Margarita*, the Old Persian name meaning "Pearl"
5. Janet	of Old English origin meaning "God's gracious gift"
6. Patricia	derived from the Latin word *Patrician* meaning "Noble"
7. Carol	originally an Old German man's name meaning "Freeman"
8. Elizabeth	of Hebrew origin meaning "God is my oath"
9. Mary	from Latin meaning "Star of the sea"
10. Anne	of Hebrew origin meaning "The gracious one"

Top 10 Boys' Baby Names [2]

1. David	corruption of the Hebrew name *Dawid* meaning "beloved"
2. John	of Hebrew origin meaning "God is Gracious"
3. Stephen	of Greek origin meaning "Garland or crown"
4. Michael	of Hebrew origin meaning "One who is like God"
5. Peter	of Greek and biblical origin meaning "Rock"
6. Robert	from Old German meaning "Bright Fame"
7. Paul	from Latin meaning "Small" or "Humble"
8. Alan	from the Celtic for "Harmony" or "Noble"
9. Christopher	of Greek origin meaning "Bearer of Christ"
10. Richard	from Old German meaning "Powerful leader"

[1] [2] Data compiled by the Office for National Statistics 1954

Games, Toys and Pastimes

After school, playing outside was a big feature of a child's life in the fifties. There were fewer cars around and the streets close to home felt safe. So, leaving with mothers' "You'd better be in by six" ringing in their ears, kids went out to play. Often, improvised balls were used to play football and cricket with jumpers for goalposts and an upturned crate for a wicket. Other popular games were hopscotch, if chalk was at hand, and tag. The more boisterous, mainly boys, would play British Bulldog, a variation of the Indian game Kabaddi, while girls would play with hula hoops and skipping ropes. The toy of the year was Mr Potato Head, a collection of plastic pieces that could be attached to a potato to make a face. As it was American, it would take a few years to reach the UK. Card games such as Happy Families were popular. It was every girl's dream to own a doll's house and every boy's to have a train set, but times were hard and it was only the lucky few who had their wishes fulfilled.

Playing out in the street

In 1952 certain foods were still being rationed following the war so the evening meal would often be a simple affair. Sugar, for example, was rationed until 1953 with meat rationing ending in 1954. Refrigeration was still a luxury most could not afford so, more often than not, food would be bought daily.

Pictured is Margaret Jones at her home in North Wales. She is collecting a plate of homemade butter from the scullery ready for the evening meal.

Mr. Davidson is seen writing a letter to his sister who lives in the United States. Writing bureaus were sought after pieces of furniture in the 1950s, often being passed down the generations as family heirlooms.

Relaxing in their armchairs in the front room of their house are teachers Mr. and Mrs. Samuel from Ebbw Vale. To the right is the tiled fireplace, a focal point for the family to gather around. The hearth is also a particular favourite for the family cat, Shan.

Dick Parry, toymaker, shows some of his Christmas toys to his children at the family home in Shrewsbury. Toy trains and doll houses featured heavily on the Christmas lists of fifties children.

Lucienne Day, pictured here, with her Calyx fabric pattern. This design generated a new school of pattern-making which became known as the 'Contemporary' style.

The Birth of Modern Design

By the 1950s Britain was slowly emerging from the privations of the Great Depression of the 1930s and from the 1940s which were overshadowed by war and its resultant shortages. The 1950s slowly became the age of the consumer and in the home it was very much "out with the old and in with the new." The 1950s was also an age when the political parties competed with each other to build new public housing. The Prime Minister Winston Churchill summoned the Housing Minister, Harold Macmillan, and tasked him with matching the previous Labour Government's achievement of building 200,000 new homes each year. These houses were smaller than pre-war homes, so furniture had to stack or be light enough to move around. Earlier inventions like serving trolleys, collapsible ironing boards and sofa beds became more commonplace. Nowhere could change be better seen than in the kitchen. Cottage style kitchens were replaced with sleek new fitted kitchens and for many the pantry was replaced by a refrigerator for the first time.

The 1950s were also a time of great design and the most enduring furniture was created by the husband and wife team of Charles and Ray Eames who produced stylish plywood, plastic and leather furniture. Another husband and wife team who brought elegance and colour into the home were Robin and Lucienne Day. Lucienne was the most influential British textile designer of the age. Her most famous design, Calyx, was created as a furnishing fabric and was used on the furniture designed by her husband. It was an abstract pattern composed of cup-shaped motifs joined by spindly lines and is one of the most recognisable and iconic designs of the 1950s.

Cawl

Cawl is a traditional hearty Welsh dish made of lamb and any vegetables available. It was popular in 1952 as it was cheap, tasty and easy to make. There were many variations of the recipe and these were handed down through the generations. Very often a secret ingredient was mentioned and, whether present or not it, added to the appeal of the meal.

Often the trick was to cook the dish the day before to allow the flavours to develop and the meat to soften. In some areas of Wales, Cawl is served in a wooden bowl and eaten with a wooden spoon with chunks of homemade bread and Welsh cheese.

Recipe (Serves 6)

The ingredients can be varied according to which vegetables are in season.

Ingredients

- 2lb Welsh lamb, middle neck or shoulder on the bone
- 1 onion, roughly chopped
- 6 medium potatoes, peeled and chopped
- 3 carrots, peeled and chopped
- 2 parsnips, peeled and chopped
- 2 leeks, washed and shredded
- 1 small bunch fresh parsley
- Vegetable stock
- Mature Caerphilly cheese, to serve

Method: Place the meat in a large heavy saucepan, cover with water and slowly bring to the boil. Simmer for 2-3 hours over a low heat. Remove from the heat and leave overnight to cool. The following morning skim off any fat that has risen to the surface. Cut the meat off the bone and return to the saucepan. Then add the vegetables, barring the leeks, and enough stock to cover them and simmer until soft. Season with salt and pepper. Before serving add the shredded leeks and parsley and put the cheese in a bowl for the diners to crumble over the stew. Enjoy.

Pineapple Upside-Down Cake

Puddings were an essential part of dinner time in 1950s Britain, with some remembered more fondly than others. Jam roly-poly, tapioca, semolina, rice pudding, stewed fruit and custard or just plain old jelly and ice cream; all could follow the main meal. For something fancier, perhaps when having guests or family to dinner, a pineapple upside down cake made for a spectacular centrepiece. Tinned pineapples rings were relatively cheap and the number used was governed by the number in the tin. Small tins had 4 rings, large tins 7 or 8.

Recipe (Serves 8)

Ingredients

For the cake: 7 pineapple rings (tinned)
7 glacé cherries
4oz softened butter
4oz caster or demerara sugar
2 large eggs or 3 small ones
4oz self raising flour
¼ teaspoon vanilla extract (optional)

For the sauce:
2oz butter, plus extra for greasing
3oz caster or demerara sugar

Method: Preheat the oven to gas mark 4/ 350 F. Lightly grease the baking tin. Melt 2oz butter and 3oz sugar in a pan and stir until combined. Pour the mixture into the tin, then arrange the pineapple rings on top, popping a cherry into the centre of each ring. Beat the remaining butter and sugar together until light and fluffy. Then beat in the eggs one at a time, beating well with each addition. Add a tablespoon of flour with the second egg (or third one if you are using small ones). Beat in the vanilla extract (if using) then fold in the remaining flour. Spoon the mixture carefully into the cake tin and spread evenly over the pineapple and cherries. Bake in the centre of the oven for 35 minutes or until the cake is springy to the touch Allow the cake to cool in the tin for five minutes before turning out onto a plate. Serve warm with cream, ice cream or custard.

Undaunted by the situation these pocket-sized models are demonstrating the latest look for children at a fashion show.

Although introduced in the mid-1940s, the modern bikini was still very controversial and met with considerable social resistance. However in the early 1950s stars such as Brigitte Bardot played a large part in bringing the bikini into the mainstream.

Ladies wearing lavish ball gowns, two with intricate embroidered floral patterns.

This elegant dress is set off with a fitted black waist belt and matching shoes.

Three types of beach/ nautical themed summer dresses. Geometric patterns would became a 1950s design hallmark.

On location in Switzerland, film star Audrey Hepburn is pictured wearing a popular linen dress style with the fashionable tight fitting waist belt.

The 1950's saw the rise of the sports jacket or sports coat for men. These patterned jackets were designed to be worn without matching trousers. Corduroy, suede, leather, denim and tweed were popular fabrics.

Father and son modelling formal coats for the winter. Trousers were loose fitting whilst Homburg hats remained popular.

The Great British Seaside Holiday

Thanks to the Holiday With Pay Act of 1938, Britons were allowed an annual paid holiday, although this gave them a measly week off per year. In 1952 those working in factories would often all have to take their holidays at the same time as production was halted in the summer. Better employers gave their workers two weeks. Only one in fifteen people ventured abroad, as few had the means to afford foreign travel. Popular destinations were those that could be reached by ferry such as France, Ireland, Holland and Belgium, although visitors to Ireland were swollen by the Irish population in Britain going home to visit family.

Relaxing by the swimming pool

A day trip to the seaside was very popular

Italy was a popular longer haul destination, but this would normally involve a flight, which would double the cost of the holiday. So for most a holiday meant one thing, a train journey to the Great British seaside, which was in its heyday. There were three main options as to where to stay. First, the guest house, with its list of rules about breakfast time and when you could use your room. Secondly, there were many holiday camps, some of which occupied old army barracks left over from the war. Camps such as Butlin's offered entertainment for both children and adults.

There was sandcastle building and sports and games such as tug-of-war and the three-legged races for the children. For adults there were sports and dancing. There were also competitions for the adults, including Miss Lovely Legs and Mr Knobbly Knees. The third and most cost-effective option was to stay with a relative, usually an older family member, who had retired to live by the coast. Much time was spent on the beach, if the weather allowed. In the 1950s people did not think of using sunblock and the aim was to get as tanned as possible as fast as possible.

Messing around in the diving competition

A bucket and spade holiday

Very often tanning accelerators were used and were homemade concoctions. One such potion was created by mixing vegetable oils with puréed carrots. In order to get and show off your tan, bathing costumes were needed. Women were increasingly sporting a bikini, a two-piece swimsuit which had been designed by the Parisian fashion house of Jacques Heim. Men would sport shorts or trunks. Many children of the era have strong memories of wearing knitted woollen costumes, often created by a generous auntie. This would act like a sponge when the children entered the water and then get filled with sand on the beach. Upon drying they would then take on the composition of cement and become extremely uncomfortable.

Father Christmas arrives by train to hand out presents to an awaiting gathering of families

Two excited children opening their presents with their mother and grandfather watching over

Christmas and Hogmanay 1952

In Scotland the celebration of Christmas was muted in the 1950s. A dispute between the Calvinist Church of Scotland and the Catholic Church of Rome saw Christmas celebrations effectively banned for 400 years. Shops were not decorated and even Christmas trees and decorations in the home were few and far between. The fact that Christmas Day did not become a public holiday until 1958, meant the day was much like any other in Scotland. The Scots instead saved all their revelry for New Year – Hogmanay. There were several traditions and superstitions that had to be taken care of before midnight. The house had to be cleaned and ashes from the fire taken out on New Year's Eve. At the stroke of midnight someone, usually a dark haired man, would bring coal, shortbread and possibly a wee dram of whisky into the house, in a tradition known as first-footing. Then the party would well and truly begin with a rendition of Robert Burns' *Auld Lang Syne*.

South of the border Christmas was celebrated with more gusto. Houses were adorned with trees and paper-chains, which were often homemade. Cards from relatives, neighbours and friends would be hung on string. Many would contain letters and might be the only written communication all year. The celebrations in 1952 were particularly special as Christmas Day fell on a Thursday, meaning that the combined holiday of that and Boxing Day gave those who did not work at weekends a four day break. Christmas Eve was a time of particular excitement for children. They were encouraged to go to their beds by the promise of a visit from Father Christmas. A mince pie and an alcoholic beverage were put out for him in preparation for his arrival. Many over-excited children slept with one eye open and noticed that Father Christmas bore more than a passing resemblance to their own father. They would wake up in the morning to the sight of a Christmas stocking or a pillow case, which contained assorted presents and the ubiquitous satsuma. As with today the Christmas dinner took centre stage. Turkey had not yet become the meat of choice and chicken was too expensive. Instead beef was a staple for most. Britain was still in a time of austerity and many people grew their own vegetables, so the trimmings were abundant and of high nutritional value. The dinner was usually timed to finish before, or start after, the monarch's Christmas Broadcast. 1952 marked Queen Elizabeth II's very first Christmas message, broadcast only on the radio at 3pm (it was first televised in 1957). Families gathered around the wireless to listen in silence to Her Majesty.

In 1952 the cinema-going experience improved greatly with the arrival of Cinerama. The process used three projectors and a wide, deeply curved screen. It gave audiences a greater sense of immersion and proved extremely popular. It was expensive though and it took years to reach most audiences. Cinema attendance fell by a quarter from its wartime peak of 1.6 million, as there was simply more to do; theatres were all open and not only was television restored after its wartime hiatus, many more people had sets at home. The 24th Oscar ceremony, honouring the best films of 1951, were presented by Danny Kaye.

A state-of-the-art curved Cinerama screen

Excerpt from A Streetcar Named Desire

Humphrey Bogart scooped the Best Actor award for his role in *The African Queen*, in doing so becoming the last man born in the 19th Century to win a leading role Oscar. Vivien Leigh won the Best Actress award for her role as Blanche Dubois in *A Streetcar Named Desire*. In theatre, October saw the premier of Agatha Christie's *The Mousetrap* at the Royal Theatre in Nottingham. The critic of the Daily Telegraph called it "The cleverest murder mystery of the British theatre, I think *The Mousetrap* could run forever". They were nearly right, it ran uninterrupted until March 2020. In popular music, courtesy of New Musical Express, Britain had its first music charts.

Their less than scientific approach saw journalists phone up a fixed number of record stores in London to enquire of their weekly sales. This had two main drawbacks. Firstly the charts were London-centric; secondly, when record producers found out which record stores were used in the sample, it left the charts open to manipulation. In classical music the composer Benjamin Britten started work on *Gloriana, Opus 53*, which paid homage to Elizabeth I. Its premiere was attended by the newly crowned Queen Elizabeth II shortly after her coronation in 1953. In March, in Cleveland, USA, the first true rock and roll festival, *The Moondog Coronation Ball*, ended in violence when the police halted the event.

Composer Benjamin Britten

Singin' in the Rain

Starring Gene Kelly, Donald O'Connor and Debbie Reynolds
Directed by Gene Kelly and Stanley Donen
Released March 27th 1952 in New York

Singin' in the Rain is a musical masterpiece, one of those unforgettable movies that the viewers never tire of watching. The cast is stellar with the film brim full of wonderful performances. It is set in 1927 and its central theme is the transition from silent cinema to the era of the talkie. Gene Kelly plays Don Lockwood, a former stuntman who forms a successful partnership with his best friend Cosmo Brown, played by Donald O'Connor. Jean Hagan plays the role of Lina Lamont, a star of the silent era who is now held back by having a grating voice. When Cosmo and Don decide to dub her with the voice of Kathy, an aspirant actress played by Debbie Reynolds, all hell breaks loose. Although the plot is interesting enough it always plays second fiddle to the song and dance routines. The film's most famous scene is one of the most memorable and most parodied in cinema history when Gene Kelly, umbrella in hand, sings the title song, *Singin' in the Rain*. Depicted as a night scene in the film it was actually filmed during the daytime on the outside film lot in Culver City. Studio technicians covered two city blocks with black tarpaulin to create the night-time effect. Multiple overhead water sprayers were installed to create the rain despite the local area suffering a severe water shortage at the time.

The Quiet Man

Starring John Wayne and Maureen O'Hara
Directed by John Ford
Released June 6th 1952 in London and Dublin

Having left Ireland as a young child Sean Thornton, played by John Wayne, returns from Pittsburgh with a view to settling down. On the way to his old home town he sees Mary Kate, a beautiful flame-haired maiden played by Maureen O'Hara, and immediately takes a shine to her. Yet even though the feeling is mutual her older brother Will, played by Victor McLaglen, develops an instant dislike to Thornton when he discovers that Sean bought the land he wanted for himself. Will is known far and wide for his fighting skills, but what nobody in Ireland knows is that Sean used to be a professional boxer in America and can more than take care of himself. As the action unfolds the film reveals itself to be the perfect blend of romance, action and drama, with some slapstick comedy thrown in for good measure.

John Ford won the Best Director Oscar for the film but John Wayne failed to even be nominated for Best Actor. His lack of even a trace of an Irish accent probably held him back. *The Quiet Man* was the second of five films where John Wayne starred alongside Maureen O'Hara. The others were *Rio Grande* (1950), *The Wings of Eagles* (1957), *McLintock* (1963) and *Big Jake* (1971).

The Snows of Kilimanjaro

Starring Gregory Peck, Ava Gardner and Susan Hayward
Directed by Henry King
Released September 17th 1952 in New York

In Africa, close to the base of Mount Kilimanjaro, Henry Street, a writer played by Gregory Peck, lies stricken with a serious leg injury. With his female companion Helen, played by Susan Hayward, he waits for transportation to hospital. Street soon develops a fever and begins to hallucinate. While feverish he remembers his life and relationships with his three loves. The film then plays out in a series of flashbacks. First we are taken to Paris where we meet Cynthia, played by Ava Gardner, and we learn that she was the love of his life. After travelling with her to Africa and Spain she leaves him, breaking his heart. He then has a dalliance with a rather cold and distant Countess, played by Hildegard Knef. Finally, in Paris on a bridge close to Notre Dame, he meets Helen, a woman who bears a striking resemblance to his true love Cynthia.

Although the main actors shot their African scenes at film studios in Hollywood, the second unit scenes were shot in Africa, Paris and Spain. These really stole the show in spectacular fashion. At the following year's Oscars, the film went on to win the award for Best Cinematography.

Peter Sellers

Down Among the Z Men

Starring Peter Sellers, Spike Milligan, Harry Secombe & Michael Bentine
Directed by Maclean Rogers
Premiered in October 1952

The Goons, who were hugely popular on radio, decided to try their hands at film with only limited success. The Z men of the title refers to an elite squadron whose job it is to guard the nation's nuclear facilities. It should come as no surprise that the four stars of the show are only enlisted due to a terrible administrative error. It then becomes a Cold War comedy of spies and secrets with mixed results. Spike Milligan does what he does best, stealing the show with his off the wall comedy. Sellers plays Colonel Bloodnok, a stiff upper lipped British officer whilst Bentine plays a mad professor who runs around in a wig, a nod to the earlier Crazy gang. The film was not a commercial success, had no general release in America and is mainly of interest to diehard Goons fans. This was the only film to feature all four original members of the Goons as Michael Bentine left the ensemble shortly afterwards. The film does have some typical Goonery lines such as "Can I try on that bathing costume in the window?" "No, you'll have to use the fitting rooms."

The Goon Show had a big impact on British and US comedy and popular culture. The Goons were cited as a major influence for the likes of The Beatles and Monty Python.

Ikiru (To live)

Starring Takashi Shimura and Miki Odagiri
Written and directed by Akira Kurosawa
Released on October 9th 1952

Ikiru is a Japanese language film loosely based on Leo Tolstoy's 1886 novella *The Death of Ivan Ilyich*. The overriding message from this movie is that it is never too late to live. Set in post-war Japan it centres around Kanji Watanabe (Takashi Shimura), a bureaucrat and chief of the City Hall, who finds out that he is terminally ill. While dying, he searches for the meaning of life, and fights for the construction of a playground in a poor area of the city as the legacy of his existence.

Ikuru is probably Kurosawa's most intimate film, inviting the viewer into the private lives of ordinary people in 1950s Japan. The performance of Takashi Shimura is both amazing and heartbreaking, in the role of a man who finds out, almost too late, that he has achieved nothing.

Director Akira Kurosawa is most often associated with samurai films but for many critics this contemporary film is his finest work. It was awarded the prestigious Silver Bear at the 1954 Berlin International Film Festival.

Limelight

Starring Charlie Chaplin and Claire Bloom
Directed and written by Charlie Chaplin
Released on October 23rd 1952

Charles Chaplin plays Calvero, a washed-up clown, who saves a ballet dancer called Terry, played by Claire Bloom, from killing herself. These two become close friends and Calvero gets meaning into his life. He desperately tries to make a comeback to become the greatest clown again, but it's hard to make people laugh any more. *Limelight* was Chaplin's last American film. It was also his most sentimental and autobiographical. Chaplin is amazing as the ageing clown and proved that he was not only a great comedian but also a terrific actor. Claire Bloom's performance as the ballet dancer is also convincing. This is a family movie in every sense of the word as Chaplin's children Sydney, Victoria, Michael, Josephine, Geraldine and Charles Jr. all pop up. There is also a cameo from another "silent" great, Buster Keaton, in a scene at the end of the film where they clown around together. This alone is worth the admission money. The film was heavily boycotted upon release in the US due to Chaplin's alleged communist sympathies. However, it was re-released in 1972 when Chaplin won his only competitive Oscar for composing the score. He also received an honorary Oscar for his contribution to film at the same ceremony receiving a standing ovation that lasted 12 minutes; the longest in Oscar's history.

In 1952 TV ownership was rare. Many people bought or rented television sets in anticipation of the broadcasting of the Queen's Coronation due to take place in June of the following year. It was not until 1958 that over half the population had a telly. In the early 50s most people relied on the radio for entertainment and information. Some programmes such as *Workers' Playtime* ,which began during WW2, were still running from 'a factory somewhere in England'. A few well-known performers would turn up at a factory canteen to perform live to the workers. Singers, accompanied on the piano, would perform in between comedy turns such as Arthur Askey, Tommy Trinder and Ted Ray. All were masters of their craft.

Tommy Trinder (with Jean Colin)

Desmond Carrington, a presenter of Housewives' Choice

Morning radio was heavily slanted towards stay-at-home wives and mothers as career women were a rarity. Programmes included *Housewives' Choice*, *Music While You Work* and *Mrs. Dale's Diary*, an early soap opera. The afternoon radio was more relaxing whilst at lunchtime there would be a light drama almost every day. This was seen as a time for the hard working housewife to put her feet up before the children came home from school and the husband from work. Band shows were still thriving at the weekend with Billy Cotton and Victor Sylvester leading the way. There was also *In Town Tonight* which was a national institution from 1933 to 1960. It was basically an early chat show which included reviews and celebrity gossip, tame by today's standards.

Radio also played a big part in children's lives. At school they could listen to educational programmes such as *Nature Study*, aimed at 9 to 11-year-olds, which ran from 1927 to 1965. Older children could learn languages via programmes like *Early Stages in French*, which was broadcast between 1952 and 1965. Pre-school children were treated to *Listen with Mother*, which could easily have been titled '*Sit still, Mother has something better to do*'. It filled a slot in the early afternoon at a quarter to two. The format consisted of a short story, some nursery rhymes and a sing-along. All services were provided by the BBC, the only sanctioned broadcaster of the day.

Children gather around the radio with their mother

Billy Bunter of Greyfriars School | 1952-1961

Gerald Campion as Billy Bunter

Billy Bunter, played by Gerald Campion, is a rather overweight schoolboy who gets up to all sorts of mischief. He is a boarder at the fictional public school of Greyfriars, which we are led to believe was founded by Henry VIII. Bunter falls asleep in class, steals food from the other boys and writes rude things on the blackboard. He also skips sports whenever he finds an excuse. Most of the time he is caught and punished for his misdeeds, receiving six-of-the-best from schoolmaster Mr. Quelch. Even by the standards of 1952 the story seemed dated. Production values were poor and Campion was rather unconvincing as a schoolboy. He was 32 at the beginning of the run and over 40 by the time the series was pulled. No recordings of the series are held by the BBC and are presumed lost, which is probably for the best.

Sooty | First appearance on television

Sooty with Harry Corbett

Sooty is a little yellow bear with a penchant for magic tricks. He started waving his wand and creating merry mischief on our television screens in 1952. Magician Harry Corbett "discovered" Sooty on Blackpool Pier in 1948 and introduced him into his children's amusement routine. At that time, Sooty had the rather unimaginative name of Teddy. It was not until Corbett performed on the BBC television show *Talent Night* that Sooty was born. After several shows, producers informed Corbett that while the novel routine was entertaining, the black and white telly of the day meant that the bear was not distinct enough. Corbett decided to blacken the bear's ears with soot and Teddy became Sooty. He was later joined by Sweep, his foil, and then Sue on the piano.

Watch with Mother | 1952-1975

Bill and Ben, The Flower Pot Men pictured in 1984 on Blue Peter with Janet Ellis

Watch with Mother was a television version of radio's *Listen with Mother*. In 1952 it saw the debut of Bill and Ben, two identical "flower pot men." The show was aimed at pre-school children and featured a common theme. An adult human gardener would go for his tea and the Flower Pot Men would come to life. Their bodies were made of flower pots, their hands of gardening gloves and their vocabulary consisted only of the words "flibadobs" and "flobadobs." The Flower Pot Men had two companions: Slowcoach the tortoise and Little Weed. The latter would alert the men to the imminent return of the gardener by squealing the words "little weed." The secret of the show's success was that children could imagine a world without adult control. Only they could see the garden come to life allowing them to delve into a magical imaginary world.

Jo Stafford

You Belong To Me

Performed by Jo Stafford

Written by Chilton Price (and possibly Redd Stewart and Pee Wee King)

Chilton Price was a music librarian at a radio station in Louisville, Kentucky. In her spare time she wrote songs which she would hand over to Stewart and Pee Wee. They would work on the arrangement and often revise the lyrics. The greatest song to emerge from this collaboration was *You Belong to Me*. The original version was recorded by Sue Thompson on Mercury's country label with another version, sung by Patti Page, making the top ten on the US Billboard Charts. By far the most successful cover was sung by Jo Stafford. Her version hit the American charts in August, and remained there for 24 weeks. In the UK, it later hit the number one spot making Stafford the first female artist to top the charts. Later, Chilton Price claimed that the she should have had solo writing credits, but was pressured by Stewart and King to include them.

Vera Lynn

Auf Wiederseh'n Sweetheart

Performed by Vera Lynn

Written by Eberhard Stroch

When Vera Lynn first heard the song, which was popular in the beer cellars of Switzerland, she felt compelled to sing an English version. The original was written in German and dedicated to the writer's wife who was ill in hospital. Lynn, the Forces Sweetheart, successfully captured the reminiscence of war efforts and soldiers leaving home by recording the song with airmen and soldiers of Her Majesty's Armed Forces. The lyrics harked back to her greatest wartime song, *We'll Meet Again*, released a decade earlier. The lyrics and sentiment are even strikingly similar as she sings "Auf Wiedersehen, auf Wiedersehen, we'll meet again sweetheart." The song was a massive hit, selling 12 million copies worldwide. She was the first overseas artist to reach number one in the US charts, staying there for 9 weeks; a record for a female artist that was only broken by Whitney Houston's *I Will Always Love You* in 1992.

Bill Haley

Icy Heart/Rock the Joint

Performed by Bill Haley and the Saddlemen

Written by Harold Bagby

It is rare that a "B" side has had such a profound effect on the history of music. Until 1952 Bill Haley had been performing a mixture of folk, country and rockabilly. The "A" side of this record, *Icy Heart*, very much followed in this pattern. Haley later described putting *Rock the Joint*, a cover of a 1949 Jimmy Preston song, on the reverse side as an afterthought. Soon radio stations would only broadcast the "B" side, hence Rock'n'Roll was born. Haley belted out the lyrics "We're gonna rock, we're gonna roll. Tear down the mailbox, rip up the floor, smash out the windows and knock down the door." The lyrics resonated with the feelings of rebellious teenagers in the US at the time; although quite what he had against mailboxes remains a mystery. In September Bill Haley changed the name of his backing band to The Comets possibly to sound like Halley's Comet.

Nat King Cole

Unforgettable

Sung by Nat King Cole (born Nathaniel Adams Coles)
Written by Irving Gordon
Released as part of his album "Unforgettable" in 1952

The song's original working title was *Undeniable*, but record producers felt that this was too clunky for the silky smooth voice of Nat King Cole. Once changed, it was difficult to imagine any other title. Cole was at the height of his fame when two versions of the song were produced. The first was a rather overblown orchestral version arranged by Nelson Riddle; the other a more tender, non-orchestrated version. The tastes of the time meant that the first version was favoured by the public. In 1991, twenty six years after his death, Elvis Presley's musical director Joe Guercio remastered the song and recorded a "virtual duet" with Cole's daughter Natalie. The song reached number 14 in the US charts; the same position it had reached forty years earlier.

Al Martino

Here in My Heart

Sung by Al Martino
Written by Pat Genaro, Lou Levinson and Bill Borrelli

When Al Martino's friend and fellow crooner Mario Lanza decided not to record the song, it was both a blessing and a curse. It would give Martino a number one single on both sides of the Atlantic. It was the first official UK number one in the newly created New Musical Express charts. It cemented his place in the record books as well as being the answer in many a pub quiz. The bad luck was that his success brought the attention of the mafia who muscled in on his management team. The mob's threat was so potent that Martino feared for his life and would not return to America for seven years. The "B" side, *I Cried Myself to Sleep Last Night*, could not have been more appropriate.

Bing Crosby

The Isle of Innisfree

Sung by Bing Crosby
Written by Dick Farrelly

Bing Crosby, whose mother was of Irish descent, recorded what was to become one of the most famous Irish folk songs of its generation. The song has a haunting melody and lyrics that express the longing of an Irish immigrant for his native land. The sentiment within the song is timeless and universal, expressing the trauma of separation from one's homeland and the joy of returning to the soil from which one is sprung. The melody, though uncredited, is the main musical theme of the film *The Quiet Man*, most notably when Maureen O'Hara and John Wayne kiss. It even features in the Spielberg classic *E.T. the Extra-Terrestrial*. The Crosby recording peaked at number 3 in the UK charts in December 1952.

Guy Mitchell

Feet Up (Pat Him on the Po-Po)

Sung by Guy Mitchell

Written by Bob Merrill

It did not take long for the fledgling UK music charts to suffer its first novelty hit. Singer and actor Guy Mitchell, an American, had great success in both the US and the UK. The writer, Bob Merrill, was to write for many great stage musicals including *Funny Girl*. This may not have been their greatest collaboration but it caught the imagination of the public, reaching number 2 in the UK charts.

The song tells of a down at heel man who is seeking to reform in order to set an example to his newborn son. The title refers to the practice of spanking a newborn child to ensure that it draws breath. It is likely that many of the British public ignored the true meaning of the song and focused on the chorus; after all we all seemed to enjoy a good *Carry On* film.

Mario Lanza

Because You're Mine

Sung By Mario Lanza (born Alfredo Arnold Cocozza)

Written by Nicholas Brodszky and Sammy Cahn

This song was released by both Lanza and Nat King Cole this year. Lanza had by far the greater success, probably because he starred in the film of the same name. The film was popular, although critics thought that Lanza's singing ability far outweighed his acting skills.

The song speaks of a man's love for a woman and is tender but a little over dramatic. Lyrics such as "I know for as long as I may live, I'll only live for the kiss that you alone may give," are followed by "And when we kiss, that isn't thunder dear, its my poor heart you hear and its applause, because you're mine."

Tony Brent

Walkin' to Missouri

Sung by Tony Brent

Written by Bob Merrill

Tony Brent, born Reginald Hogan Bretagne in Bombay, enjoyed a short but successful career with seven Top 20 hits in the 1950s. This cover of a popular Bob Merrill song is an allegorical story of a young man (the robin), who is lured by the bright lights and promises of the big city. There he falls for a girl and is betrayed by her. She has been having an affair with another for the whole time. He ends up losing everything, and "penniless" he walks back to his small home town in Missouri. "Poor little robin. Walkin' walkin' walkin' to Missouri, he can't afford to fly. Got a penny for poor little robin? Walkin' walkin' walkin' to Missouri. Got a teardrop in his eye." It peaked at number 7 in the UK charts.

The Very First UK Music Chart

Published on 14th November 1952 by the New Musical Express this was the first authentic weekly survey of the bestselling pop records from leading gramophone record retailers. For this first chart there were 12 records in the Top 10 as there were 2 tied positions.

1	**Here In My Heart** Al Martino		**7**	**Forget-Me-Not** Vera Lynn
2	**You Belong To Me** Jo Stafford		**7**	**High Noon** Frankie Laine
3	**Somewhere Along The Way** Nat King Cole		**8**	**Sugar Bush** Doris Day / Frankie Laine
4	**Isle Of Innisfree** Bing Crosby		**8**	**Blue Tango** Ray Martin/Leroy Anderson
5	**Feet Up** Guy Mitchell		**9**	**Homing Waltz** Vera Lynn
6	**Half As Much** Rosemary Clooney		**10**	**Auf Wiederseh'n Sweetheart** Vera Lynn

Billboard year-end Top 10 singles of 1952

Over in the USA these were the 10 bestselling records of the year:

1	**Blue Tango** Leroy Anderson		**6**	**Half As Much** Rosemary Clooney
2	**Wheel Of Fortune** Kay Starr		**7**	**Wish You Were Here** Eddie Fisher
3	**Cry** Johnnie Ray & The Four Lads		**8**	**I Went To Your Wedding** Patti Page
4	**You Belong To Me** Jo Stafford		**9**	**Here In My Heart** Al Martino
5	**Auf Wiederseh'n Sweetheart** Vera Lynn		**10**	**Delicado** Percy Faith

The World's First Rock and Roll Concert

The Moondog Coronation Ball on March 21st 1952 in Cleveland, Ohio.

The "Moondog" in question was the legendary disc jockey Alan Freed, the self-styled "father of rock and roll", who was the then host of the enormously popular "Moondog Show" on a local radio station. His friend, record shop owner Leo Mintz, told him of the growing popularity amongst customers of all races for rhythm and blues records by black artists.

Mintz decided to sponsor a three-hour, late-night programme presented by Freed. The programme proved enormously popular with advertising revenues pouring into the station's coffers. It was then that Mintz and Freed decided to do something that had never before been done: hold a live music event featuring many of the acts who were featured on the show.

Disc Jockey Alan Freed

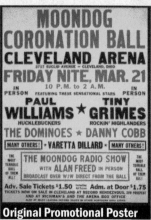

Original Promotional Poster

Dubbed "The Moondog Coronation Ball," the event was to feature headliners Paul Williams and his Hucklebuckers and Tiny Grimes and the Rocking Highlanders (a black instrumental group who performed in Scottish kilts). In the end, however, the incredible demand for tickets proved to be the event's undoing.

Not helped by overselling and counterfeiting, more than 25,000 people turned up to a venue that only had a capacity for 10,000, meaning that 15,000 were held outside as the concert began. After one hour of the proposed three-hour show the crowd outside broke through the gates causing the police to move in swiftly to stop the show. Many felt that the police were looking for an excuse to halt it as the authorities were uncomfortable with racially mixed audiences in segregated America.

Although it cannot be described as a success the "Moondog Coronation Ball" entered the record books as the first rock and roll concert.

Chaotic scenes at the overcrowded venue

Headline artist Tiny Grimes

The Royal Variety Performance on November 3rd 1952 at The London Palladium

in the presence of Her Majesty Queen Elizabeth II and His Royal Highness the Duke of Edinburgh

The new Queen's first Variety Performance was greeted with much anticipation and some nervousness. The show featured a roll-call of the great and the good from British radio, stage and screen as well as a few acts from further afield. Bud Flanagan had the honour of warming up the audience, and much like a court jester of old he had to make a joke about the monarch without insulting them. He pitched it perfectly with his line "and don't look up to see if the Queen is laughing first, or you'll get on her bleeding nerves". The Queen and the audience were able to laugh together. Applause rang around the Palladium as Gerry Brereton, who had been blinded in the Second World War, took to the stage unaided and sang *Here in My Heart*. Crowd favourite Gracie Fields, who made her performance debut some 24 years earlier, then came on to perform a duet with Italian tenor Beniamino Gigli. Together they sang *Come Back to Sorrento*.

Gracie Fields

Terry-Thomas

Fields was frightened that her raunchy style would be too much for the Queen and her toned down act left critics yearning for her honest-to-goodness vulgarity. Although not listed on the programme, there was a surprise appearance by Maurice Chevalier who was performing a summer show at the nearby Hippodrome. He was introduced to the audience as "the idol of French music hall". Ted Ray, Arthur Askey, Norman Wisdom, Terry-Thomas and the Crazy Gang kept the laughs coming thick and fast. The comedy was interspersed with musical offerings from Winifred Atwell, the Beverley Sisters and Vera Lynn. From overseas came artists like the American comedian Vic Oliver, Australian juggler Rob Murray, who muttered under his breath all through his act, and Nancy Crompton who travelled all the way from New York to dance at the show for 3 minutes.

The undoubted star of the show was the troubled genius Tony Hancock. In a story related by Bill Pertwee, Hancock was sharing a dressing room with other comedians including Norman Wisdom and Ted Ray. Sitting at his dressing table, Hancock applied his make-up slowly whilst helping himself to a glass of brandy every few minutes. After watching for a while, Wisdom had a word and told Hancock to slow down as it might affect his performance. In reply, Hancock said that he was alright and poured himself another glass. When his call came, he left the others in the dressing room anxiously waiting for the tannoy to relay his act from the stage. They needn't have worried, Hancock left the stage to thunderous applause. His routine, which was a parody of a naval commander, was particularly well received by the Duke of Edinburgh, himself a commander during the war. Hancock returned to the dressing room to be greeted by overjoyed friends. However he was unmoved by their praise, finished off the bottle of brandy, put on his coat and went to a pub across the road before returning to join the final curtain call.

Norman Wisdom

The Nobel Prize in Literature was won by Bordeaux-born François Mauriac for his body of work which included novels, plays, literary criticism and journalism. He had been a member of the French Resistance during the Second World War. In America, The Pulitzer Prize for Fiction was won by Herman Wouk for his book *The Cain Mutiny*. In Britain, Agatha Christie produced three novels, *Mrs. McGinty's Dead*, *They Do It with Mirrors* and *A Daughter's A Daughter*. These gave fresh airings to two of her stock characters, the insouciant Hercule Poirot and the redoubtable Miss Jane Marple. With the war still fresh in the memory, Alan Bullock produced one of the finest biographies of Adolph Hitler in his book *Hitler: A Study in Tyranny*. It not only analysed the mind of a deranged dictator but also the system that was allowed to evolve around him. It became a go-to textbook for many schoolchildren and university students for many decades.

Author François Mauriac

Poet Laureate John Masefield

The Poet Laureate, John Masefield, was in contemplative mood as the early fifties was a barren spell for him. His biggest legacy from the period can be found in the form of letters to Greta Stevens which he wrote from 1952 to 1965. In them he discusses the work of other poets, notably W.B. Yeats. In the visual arts, Frank Auerbach started a remarkable series of sketches. He became fascinated by the building sites of London that sprang up during the reconstruction after the war. When he returned to his studio, he would turn them into paintings, working and reworking them until the paint was over an inch deep, acting as a metaphor for post-war reconstruction.

In France, Pablo Picasso commenced work on a wall painting on the theme of war and peace in a 14th century chapel. It would take him five years to complete. On the other side of the Atlantic, Georgia O'Keeffe produced another desert masterpiece with her *Mesa and Road East*. Freda Kahlo was experimenting with Primitive Art and produced *Congress for Peoples of Peace*, an optimistic work in light of the Cold War between the Capitalist West and the Communist East. In sculpture, Henry Moore produced one of his most iconic works, *Upright Internal/External Form*, where he explored the themes of birth and rebirth. The initial work was done in plaster to be recast in bronze. A twenty feet high version stood in the atrium of the Three First National Plaza in Chicago until it was sold in 2016.

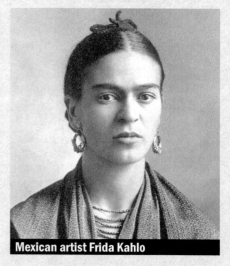
Mexican artist Frida Kahlo

Anne Frank's Diary

English language version   Published: April 30th 1952

The heart-rending diary of Anne Frank, a Jewish victim of the Holocaust, became available in British book shops entitled *The Diary of a Young Girl*. The book was first published in her native Dutch in 1947 under the title *Het Achterhuis* (The Secret House) by her father Otto Frank; he had survived the concentration camps. It is a lively, and at the same time disturbing, account of a teenager living in hiding with seven others in fear of their lives in occupied Holland. Their hiding place was raided by the Gestapo on the 4th August 1944 after a tip-off from an informer. Anne and seven other inhabitants were sent to a transit camp in Holland, and then on to Auschwitz and Bergen-Belsen. Anne died weeks before the liberation of Bergen-Belsen as did her mother, Edith, and sister, Margot. Having survived, her father returned to Amsterdam where he, his family and friends had been in hiding for two years before the Nazis found them. Whilst there, his Dutch friends gave him papers left behind after the Gestapo raid. Among them was his daughter's diary.

Charlotte's Web

Author: E.B. White   Published: October 15th 1952

The story opens with Fern Arable, an eight-year-old farm girl, stopping her father from killing a piglet which is the runt of the litter. The little pig, who Fern names Wilbur, then becomes one of the central characters of the story. Eventually he will be befriended by Charlotte, the wise and loving spider of the book's title. The book is beautifully written in simple graceful language and is probably the most accessible children's book of its time. It does however deal with difficult themes. After Charlotte lays her eggs she goes the way of most female spiders and grows weaker and weaker and dies. The story is one of loyalty, morality and ultimately redemption. After Charlotte dies, Wilbur guards her eggs until her babies are born. While most of them flee the nest, three spiders remain and become the pig's friends. He is then able to guide them the way Charlotte guided him, giving the tale a wonderful sense of continuity.

East Of Eden

Author: John Steinbeck   Published: September 19th 1952

Steinbeck was a masterful writer who in this book perfectly evokes the Salinas Valley in California of his youth. He brings the history of the place alive through his cast of many sympathetic and some hideous characters. *East of Eden* uses a plethora of Biblical analogies, starting with that in the title referring to the expulsion of Adam and Eve from The Garden of Eden. Here the central character, Adam, is expelled from his home town to be thrust into the senseless hell of World War I. Like other veterans he returns to a community that neither understands nor appreciates what he has lived through. His inability to adjust to civilian life draws him into conflict with all around him, particularly his brother Charles. Steinbeck again takes inspiration from the Old Testament, this time drawing on the story of Cain and Abel. The book explores themes of power, sexual rivalry, jealousy and family favouritism. Though it has a tragic ending, it also offers a level of redemption.

Waiting for Godot

Author: Samuel Beckett   Written in 1952, first performed on stage in 1953

Waiting for Godot is a play that asks many questions, and answers none of them. As the title suggests, it is about waiting: two tramps waiting for a third man who never appears. "And if he comes?" one of Beckett's tramps asks. "We'll be saved", the other replies. The nature of that salvation, along with so much else, remains undefined for both characters and audience. The two main characters, Vladimir and Estragon, wait for someone named Godot, who never arrives. The meaning of the name Godot has long been debated. Although Beckett wrote it in French, it is possible that he wanted his audiences to consider the significance of the English word "God" in the name. The similarity between the words Godot and God does not exist in French, in which God is "Dieu". Other theories suggest that Beckett named the character after either a French cyclist called Roger Godeau or a French slang word for boots. These sit well with what is agreed to be the central theme of the play, namely the futility of human existence.

Collected Poems 1934-1952

Author: Dylan Marlais Thomas

Dylan Thomas once famously said of the country of his birth, Wales, "The land of my fathers, my fathers can have it." Even though both his parents were Welsh speakers they brought their children up to speak only English. Thomas never learnt Welsh and always had ambivalent feelings towards Wales. He preferred New York to Swansea, but also preferred drunkenness to sobriety. This collection of poetry, which spans almost two decades, features Thomas's finest works. The poems dedicated to his father are the most poignant and also the best known. In *Do not go gentle into that good night* he compares the passage of the sun across the sky to the course of human life. He returned to the theme of his father's loss of sight and impending death in *Elegy* which opens with "Too proud to die; broken and blind he died." Thomas himself was not long for this world. A year after the release of this anthology he died aged just 39.

Voyage of the Dawn Treader

Author: Clive Staples Lewis   Published: September 5th 1952

The book has one of the cleverest opening lines in children's literature: "There was a boy named Eustace Clarence Scrubb, and he almost deserved it." *The Voyage of the Dawn Treader* was the third Narnia novel to be published (although it is the fifth chronologically in the series). Edmund & Lucy, along with their annoying cousin Eustace Scrubb, are sucked back into Narnia through a painting of a ship. Unlike most of the other Narnia stories, there is no major villain to be toppled. Instead, the children join Prince Caspian on a voyage of discovery and adventure into the unexplored eastern seas of Narnia. Along the way our heroes encounter undiscovered islands, bizarre magic, threatening sea monsters and much more. Lewis explores broad themes like courage, faith, perseverance, loyalty and morality in the face of tough choices. He had a talent for drawing out principled lessons in life, for young and old readers alike.

The Borrowers

Author: Mary Norton   Published: 1952 (in USA: 1953)

Arrietty Clock and her parents, Pod and Homily, are tiny people who live beneath the floorboards of an old house and 'borrow' the things they need from the full-sized people who live in the house above. At one point many borrowers lived in the house, but the others left for various reasons leaving only the Clocks. While her parents seem happy, Arrietty longs to see the world outside. Her mother finally persuades Pod to take her borrowing and on her first time out, she meets the boy upstairs. The boy is as curious about Arrietty as she is about him, and they become good friends. The boy brings the family all kinds of gifts such as a cigar box to use as a bed, food and even jewellery. Unfortunately, the boy takes too much and the housekeeper notices things are missing. Soon the Clocks are forced to flee. This terrific book is about companionship, different cultures, greed and fear. The book is so well crafted that the reader believes that Borrowers really do exist.

The Old Man and the Sea

Author: Ernest Hemingway   Written in 1951, Published in 1952

This is a classic 'man versus nature' fable given poignancy because the man, Santiago, is so old and alone. He has, as described in the book's opening, "gone eighty-four days without taking a fish." Outside of an interest in baseball, fishing is his life. His one true friend, Manolin, is a boy who has been told not to fish with Santiago because he is unlucky. The novella is beautifully structured. Hemingway sets up the old man's routine at the beginning with the loyal boy helping him after another fruitless day out in his skiff, fetching him food and drink, and then bait for the next day's fishing. We can imagine that this is a routine that plays out nightly. The majority of the book takes place far out to sea, where Santiago hooks an enormous marlin, a creature who symbolically is also old. He spends the next couple of days fighting to reel it in, cutting his hands on the line while trying to eat and drink. The Old Man talks to himself, studying the water and sky whilst remembering episodes from his past.

Murder with Mirrors (also published as They Do it with Mirrors)

Author: Agatha Christie   Miss Marple book No. 5

Unusually in this Miss Marple mystery, Jane appears in the story from its very beginning. She is asked by an old friend to visit her sister at her family home, where something has her worried. So Miss Marple goes for a visit and discovers a strange living environment. There are many curious characters who flit in and out of the house. You get a sense that all can't be well and that something is about to happen. But who is the person in danger? Her friend, Carrie Louise, seems to be loved by everyone including former stepchildren but sooner or later there is a murder. There are plenty of interesting characters to worry about/suspect/feel sorry for. Part of the fun of this story is trying to figure out what is really going on. All of the clues are there plus more than a few red herrings. The queen of misdirection titled this book with an old phrase about magicians' misdirection tricks. As always, this keeps you guessing right until the very end.

The Mousetrap

The Mousetrap at St. Martin's Theatre in London pictured in 2006

Written by Agatha Christie
Premiered 6th October 1952
at the Theatre Royal Nottingham

Penned by the 'Queen of Suspense', *The Mousetrap* was adapted from a radio play titled *Three Blind Mice* written in 1947. The stage play had to be renamed as it clashed with another play written before the war. Christie's son-in-law, Anthony Hicks, suggested the new title. It refers to Shakespeare's Hamlet in which the title character calls the play depicting the murder of the king *The Mousetrap*. The scene is set when a group of people gather in a country house and are cut off by inclement winter weather. They discover, much to their horror, that there is a murderer in their midst. One by one the characters reveal their sordid pasts casting suspicions from one character to another until, at the last nerve-jangling moment, the identity of the murderer and their motives are finally revealed. When it transferred to London's West End the cast included Richard Attenborough and his wife Sheila Sim. One actor who has been included in every performance since its opening night is the late Deryck Guyler, whose voice recording reads the news in every performance. *The Mousetrap* holds the record as the longest running play in the world. With only a short enforced break in 2020/21 due to Covid the show has been performed over 28,000 times.

The Deep Blue Sea

Sir Terence Rattigan

Written by Sir Terence Rattigan
Starring Dame Peggy Ashcroft and Kenneth More
Premiered in London on March 6th 1952

Hester Collyer loves Freddie Page. She loves him so much she leaves her husband Bill to run away with Freddie to Canada, where he works as a test pilot. She loves him so much she tries to kill herself when he forgets her birthday. She loves him so much she cannot bear the thought that he does not love her as much as she loves him. So goes *"The Deep Blue Sea"*. The play starts with Hester's failed suicide attempt, which is discovered by her landlady and another tenant who smell gas. While the premise of the play may sound melodramatic, it never really goes over the line. Rattigan shows a woman who is devastated by her love for this seemingly ordinary man that makes her act in a way she never dreamed of. Here is a great story of how love can make people act irrationally and against their own best interests.

While Freddie Page could seem like an unlikeable character for not feeling the same amount of love for Hester, his honesty and integrity shine through. Ultimately the couple both know that they are bad for each other, best summed up by the line "We are death for each other" as their lives spiral out of control.

London Laughs

A review by Alec Shanks and Joan Davis
Opened on February 12th 1952
at the Adelphi Theatre, London

Vera Lynn

Tommy Cooper

London Laughs featured a veritable Who's Who of the British entertainment industry. It was a mixture of music, dance, comedy and novelty acts, much like the Royal Variety Performance of today. The production commenced with an overture by the house orchestra. This allowed the audience to settle down and latecomers to take their seats. Then the fun started with an irreverent sketch called *Blossom in Covent Garden*, a comedy and dance routine, brim full of innuendo. With the audience warmed up, it was the turn of wartime Forces Sweetheart Vera Lynn to take to the stage. However, any attempts at seriousness were thwarted by handlebar moustachioed, funny man Jimmy Edwards as she sang *Hello to You*.

London Laughs Poster

Things took a more artistic turn with *A Fantasy in Black and White*, where Lorrae Desmond was joined on stage by silhouetted dancers. Tommy Cooper then did what Tommy Cooper did best in his *Crazy Conjuring* routine, proving that he was such a good magician he could make it look bad. It was then the turn of a comedy sketch written by Frank Muir and Dennis Norden called *Polly Does Everything*. The title tells you all you need to know and it featured Jimmy Edwards most improbably as a Sheik. Vera Lynn then returned to the stage to sing a duet, *Carriage and Pair*. If by this stage the audience were flagging Edwards burst forward in schoolmasterly fashion in his skit *Wake Up Back There!* The theatregoers were then treated to a final medley of Al Jolson melodies. The cast would rotate and many of the comedians of the day would use the play as a bridge between radio and TV, most notably Tony Hancock.

Sculptors: Henry Moore & Barbara Hepworth

The similarities between the two greatest British sculptors of the twentieth century extend far beyond their work. It is more than likely that you will have seen their work in the public spaces of Britain. They were both born in Yorkshire 5 years apart and less than 10 miles from each other. They both trained at Leeds College of Art and then the Royal College of Art in London. They shared a fascination with direct carving; a technique working directly with a material rather than the more traditional method of modelling. World War II saw their paths diverge. Hepworth retreated to Cornwall where, with her husband Ben Nicholson, she joined a growing group of artists. In contrast Moore remained in Hertfordshire, closer to London thereby being more accessible to the press and the art world. As an official war artist Moore focused on sketching victims of air raids. Hepworth on the other hand drew inspiration from the natural landforms of the Cornish coast.

Reclining Figure - Henry Moore

In the late forties their paths diverged further. While Hepworth became obsessed with waves crashing onto rocks and natural forms, Moore was more influenced by the human form and primitive art. Crucially Moore worked on enormous pieces of stone and bronze, whereas Hepworth chose to work with wood and stone on a smaller scale. Moore was the vocal, confident artist that the British Council wanted to have promote British modern art, a role that did not sit well with the more introverted Hepworth. This became strikingly clear at Moore's British pavilion at the 1948 Venice Biennale which received considerable acclaim in contrast to Hepworth's more subdued exhibition two years later. Several critics even assumed that Hepworth was Moore's pupil, much to her chagrin. In 1952 Hepworth produced her greatest book, the illustrated *Carvings and Drawings*. It was her first full monograph and covered her career to that point. It is split into six distinct sections, which she introduces with her own insightful words. It covers subjects from the influence of ancient Greek architecture, to the importance of gender in her work, at a time when feminism was in its infancy. Aside from their differences, what Hepworth and Moore brought to the world was their common desire to take art out of elitist galleries and make it accessible to all, be it in open spaces or on the side of shops, such as Hepworth's *Winged Figure* which graces the side of John Lewis Oxford Street.

Single Form - Barbara Hepworth

The Arch - Henry Moore

Winged Figure - Barbara Hepworth

John Masefield, Poet Laureate (served 1930-1967)

John Masefield

Masefield was the longest serving Poet Laureate to serve entirely within the 20th century. His 37 years of service was only beaten by Alfred, Lord Tennyson who held the post between 1850-1892. By the 1950s Masefield seemed to be from a bygone era as traditional poetry had fallen out of favour as more modernist poets such as Sylvia Plath and Stevie Smith were gaining more traction. The emerging Beat Generation of poets such as Ginsburg, Carr and Huncke seemed to speak more to the youth of the day than did the rather staid Masefield. Still, he took his job seriously and acted as all good Poets Laureate do and wrote poems for the court, in his case the House of Windsor. Rather quaintly Masefield would send his poems to the Times of London for their approval with a stamped addressed envelope for their response. Even though he seemed more like a 19th century poet than most of his contemporaries, many of his poems still stand the test of time. His *Sonnets and Poems* written in the midst of World War I and *A Generation Risen* written during World War II defined him as a chronicler of British 20th century history and one of the few poets to have written during both wars. In 1952 he published his autobiography *So Long to Learn*.

The Role of Poet Laureate Through The Ages

The monarch of the day bestows the honorary position of Poet Laureate, currently on the advice of the prime minister. There are no specific duties to the role although it is expected that the holder produces original verse to commemorate significant national occasions. The first official Poet Laureate was John Dryden who was appointed by Charles II in 1668. Until Andrew Motion was appointed in 1999 the laureateship was held for life; subsequently the position has been offered for a fixed term of 10 years. Other notable Poet Laureates included William Wordsworth (1843-1850), Sir John Betjeman (1972-1984) and Ted Hughes (1984-1998). The actor Daniel Day-Lewis's father, Cecil, was also Poet Laureate from 1968 to 1972. It was only in 2009 that the first woman, Carol Ann Duffy, was offered the role. She was also the first Scot.

Sir John Betjeman

The role of Poet Laureate is not a money spinner; Andrew Motion and Carol Ann Duffy were offered annual salaries of £5,750 per year. However, in a quirky tradition dating back to Charles I, the holder also receives a barrel of sherry.

Carol Ann Duffy

Improving Everyday Life

The 1950s were a time of great inventiveness. Whereas much of the previous decade was taken up with war, the 1950s allowed scientists and creative thinkers to turn their attention to improving everyday life. Many things that we take for granted today stem from this period. Where would we be without the credit card, the passenger jet plane, the barcode and the car airbag? The video cassette recorder, though now largely redundant, changed the way we watched films and the television remote control allowed us to switch channels effortlessly. The development of the oral contraceptive gave many women more choice about if and when to start a family.

Early VCR's were very large and used open reels

The invention of the microchip, the hard drive and the early programming language FORTRAN heralded a new age in computing. There were also giant leaps in medicine. The external heart pacemaker, a device to regulate heartbeats, gave hope to millions, while the roll out of the eponymous Salk vaccine would eventually make much of the world polio-free, saving countless lives. Other inventions were less heralded, though would have a profound effect on the world and the way we see it. Polypropylene is a word that may not trip easily off the tongue, but it is the most useful plastic, used in packaging, textiles and car manufacture. Alistair Pilkington's design of float glass revolutionised the way we see in and out of buildings and the automatic sliding door changed the way we entered and exited them.

A chair made of polypropylene

In the kitchen, the non-stick frying pan made life easier, especially when cooking a fry-up. Children were treated to Mr. Potato Head, the hula hoop (although earlier versions dated back to at least 500BC) and Barbie Doll, though we would have to wait until the '60s for the appearance of Ken. Whilst most inventions were aimed at improving the lives and health of the population, one invention did not count among these and it changed the world forever. In 1952 the USA detonated the first thermonuclear device—the hydrogen bomb (H bomb). It was a thousand times more powerful than the atomic bombs dropped on Japan during the Second World War. By the end of the decade the Soviet Union, Britain and China had also tested H bombs and the age of potentially Mutually Assured Destruction (MAD) was born.

AMAZING NEW CONCEPT IN *Cooking*

FREE SPATULA WITH EACH "HAPPY PAN"

NOTHING STICKS TO "HAPPY PAN"

A cast iron skillet sealed with DuPont TEFLON®

An advert for a non-stick pan

The Story of the Comet: From Triumph to Disaster

A series 4 BEA De Havilland DH-106 Comet

Between the mid 1930s and 1950 military aircraft design advanced from propeller driven biplanes to jet powered monoplanes. Civil aviation relied on large propeller driven aircraft until 1949 when de Havilland unveiled the age of the jet airliner. Sir Geoffrey de Havilland conceived the idea of the DH106 'Comet' in 1943 and design work began in September 1946. The prototype first flew on 27th July 1949. On 2nd May 1952 the de Havilland Comet entered service with BOAC as the first commercial jet airliner. This marked a new era in civil aviation and left other aeroplane manufacturers years behind.

Comet prototype at Hatfield airfield

The engines concealed in the wing

The new aircraft could carry 36 passengers at a cruising speed of 720 km/h (450 mph) over a distance of 4000 km (2500 miles). BOAC became the envy of world airlines by operating the first jet fleet. In order to carry the maximum amount of passengers and freight, the weight of the aircraft and fuel had to be kept to a minimum. The construction techniques were a mixture of old and new: rivets were used but were also glued together using a technique known as Redux bonding. The plane featured passenger aviation innovations such as a pressurised cabin, large square windows and the jet engines concealed within the wings.

After only eighteen months of service two aircraft disappeared within three months of each other. A full investigation was carried out by the Royal Aircraft Establishment (RAE) at Farnborough. One part of the investigation examined cabin pressurisation. This used water to produce cabin loading and hydraulic rams to generate wing loading. BOAC Comet, Yoke Uncle, was placed inside a water tank with the wings protruding through seals in the walls of the tank. The skin of Yoke Uncle underwent a mix of 3057 actual and simulated flight cycles before a metal fatigue crack produced a failure at a rivet hole near the forward port escape hatch. Metal fatigue, a phenomenon not well understood at the time, is where high stresses under repeated loads can cause micro cracks to form in the airframe. It was concluded that Yoke Uncle would have suffered cabin failure at around 9000 flight hours, had it continued in service. The disasters triggered several revisions of the plane's design including the replacement of square windows with oval shaped ones. The series 4 launched in 1958 which remained in commercial service until 1981. The Comet was truly groundbreaking and jet-propelled the aviation industry into the world of air travel we know today.

The Barcode

Close up of a UPC-A barcode

One of modern life's minor irritations occurs when a barcode fails to scan at the supermarket checkout. An action that should be over in the blink of an eye then takes what seems to be an interminable amount of time. This is what life was like before the invention of the barcode and barcode scanner. In 1952 Norman Joseph Woodland, a teacher at the Drexel Institute of Technology in the USA, led a team who patented the first barcodes. It is believed that Woodland came up with the idea when he drew concentric circles in the sand (early barcodes were round, more like an archery board than the linear ones of today). Their first practical use was in industry and on the US railroad system for monitoring stock. They took a further 10 years to make their way into US shops, but when they did they not only sped up transactions, they also made stocktaking faster and more accurate. It was not until 1979 that barcodes were used in the UK at Keymarkets in Spalding, Lincolnshire. Since then they have not only revolutionised the retail sector but are used in other fields such as the NHS. Barcodes uniquely identify every patient, product and location, helping to improve safety, reduce clinical errors and improve operational efficiency, saving both money and lives.

Float Glass

The window pane top left has been replaced with float glass. Notice how blurry the tree reflection looks in the other panes

A simple experiment can be undertaken when on any street in Britain. When looking through a window whether from inside or outside, if the glass shows a distorted image then it was made before the invention of float glass. If the image is crystal clear then the window was made after it. Legend has it that in 1952, whilst doing the dishes one night, Alistair Pilkington noticed one of the plates floating on the surface of the water in the sink. In a eureka moment, it struck him that if he could float glass on a liquid surface the molten glass would produce a flat surface due to the forces of gravity. One big obstacle was yet to be overcome, he had to find the perfect liquid for floating molten glass. Water could not be used as it would evaporate upon coming into contact with the glass. Seven years research followed before, in 1959, molten tin provided the solution. Thus the Pilkington process was born, producing glass of zero distortion and amazing clarity. Its applications were almost endless. It made our private and public buildings brighter, revolutionised conservatory design and even led to an increase in food production as more sunlight could now reach crops in greenhouses.

Can a helicopter fly across the Atlantic Ocean?

The short answer is yes, but there is no practical reason to do it other than to prove that it can be done. Helicopters are far slower than aeroplanes, require more frequent refuelling and are far noisier for those on board. The noise in the cabin of an aeroplane is around 80 decibels, a little more than the sound of a vacuum cleaner. In a helicopter the crew are subjected to

A Sikorsky H-19 helicopter

100 decibels, which is the sound of a motorbike at full throttle. The first transatlantic helicopter flight took place in July 1952 when Captain Vincent H. McGovern and First Lieutenant Harold W. Moore piloted two Sikorsky H-19 helicopters over a total of 3,410 miles. Their journey began in Westover, Massachusetts on July 15th and took 16 days to reach Prestwick in Scotland. The total flying time was 42 hours 25 minutes with several stops being required over the course of the journey. In truth the two pilots did not really cross the Atlantic, but skirted around it. A great feat nonetheless.

The first non-stop transatlantic helicopter flight was achieved in 1967 between New York and Paris with the aid of in-flight refuelling.

The H Bomb

"I know not with what weapons World War III will be fought, but World War IV will be fought with sticks and stones"

Albert Einstein

The Ivy Mike test mushroom cloud

On November 1st 1952, the United States successfully detonated "Mike," the world's first hydrogen bomb, on the Eniwetok Atoll in the Pacific Marshall Islands. The 10.4-megaton thermonuclear device, built upon the Teller-Ulam principles of staged radiation implosion, instantly vaporised an entire island and left behind a crater more than a mile wide. The enormous explosive force of Mike was also apparent from the sheer magnitude of its mushroom cloud; within 90 seconds the mushroom cloud climbed to 57,000 feet and entered the stratosphere. One minute later, it reached over 100,000 feet, eventually stabilising at a ceiling of 120,000 feet. Half an hour after the test, the mushroom stretched 60 miles across, with the base of the head joining the stem at 45,000 feet. Three years later, on November 22nd 1955, the Soviet Union detonated its first hydrogen bomb on the same principle of radiation implosion. Both superpowers were now in possession of the "hell bomb," as it was known by many Americans, and the world lived under the threat of thermonuclear war for the first time in history. The world would never be the same again.

The Braeburn Apple

The Braeburn Apple

A chance seedling is a plant that is the product of unintentional breeding. One chance seedling was discovered by farmer O.Moran in the Moutere Hills in New Zealand in 1952. In this case the seedling was an apple. Farmer Moran noticed this particular apple had a red/orange vertical streaky appearance on a yellow/green background. A local nursery then cultivated the apple as a potential candidate for commercial export. This new apple which is the offspring of the Delicious and Sturmer Pippin varieties was then grown locally in the Braeburn Orchard. And so began the story one of the most popular apple varieties in the UK and the USA.

The Braeburn is particularly good for cooking as it retains its shape and doesn't release large quantities of liquid. They make a great choice for an apple tart as they have a pleasing combination of both sweet and tart flavours. However, Braeburns can sometimes suffer from a browning disorder of the flesh after longs periods of chilled storage. To combat this a further cultivar was developed in 1985 which we know today as the 'Jazz' apple.

Cinerama Widescreen Film

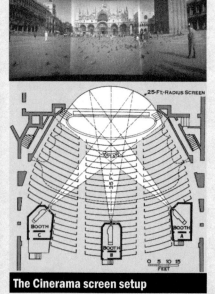

The Cinerama screen setup

The Cinerama widescreen process was the world's first commercial multi-projection cinema experience launched on the 30th September 1952 in the Broadway Theatre in New York. It uses three synchronised 35mm projectors to simultaneously project on to a giant curved screen that wraps around 146 degrees. It incorporated the world's first surround sound system allowing sounds to be targeted across seven speakers in the auditorium. This immersive sound and vision experience almost completely filled the audience's field of vision. The first film to be shown, *This is Cinerama*, made the most of this technology by giving the audience a point-of-view thrill ride on the Atom Smasher roller coaster from Rockaway's Playland in New York. Other adventures included views of Niagara Falls, the canals in Venice and a low level flight through some of the natural landmarks in the American West.

The Cinerama process was created by the prolific inventor Fred Waller. He patented a number of other inventions including a camera that could take a 360-degree photo. He also notably successfully patented the water ski in 1925.

Rosalind Franklin and Photo 51

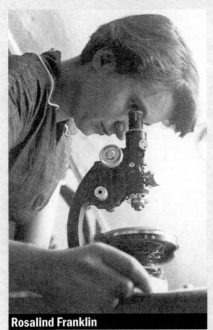

Rosalind Franklin

In 1952 whilst working at King's College London, English chemist and X-ray crystallographer Rosalind Franklin supervised a series of X-ray fibre diffraction images of a DNA fibre. The 51st image in this series was to become critical evidence in identifying the structure of DNA. Although it was James Watson and Francis Crick who would a year later publish the milestone paper proposing the double helix structure of DNA molecules, there remains controversy to this day about the lack of attribution that Rosalind Franklin received. Franklin was working with a graduate student, Raymond Gosling, at the time of the images. She was also due to leave King's College shortly after. Gosling shared the image with his new supervisor, Maurice Wilkins, who subsequently shared the image with James Watson without telling Franklin. Watson recognised the pattern as a helix which made a significant contribution to their landmark 1953 paper. Tragically Rosalind Franklin died at the age of 37 from ovarian cancer, fours year before Watson, Crick and Wilkins were awarded the Nobel Prize in 1962. Her role in the discovery was only truly recognised after her death.

Sir David Attenborough joins the BBC

Sir David Attenborough

Sir David Attenborough was born on 8th May 1926. He joined the BBC in 1952 as a trainee working first on the quiz show *Animal, Vegetable or Mineral?* In 1954 he stepped in front of the camera to host the show *Zoo Quest* which for the first time combined footage shot on location with live studio presenting. In 1965 he was appointed Controller of the newly created BBC2. He was responsible for commissioning iconic shows including *Match of the Day, The Old Grey Whistle Test* and *Monty Python's Flying Circus*. Attenborough also brought snooker to the BBC when colour television was introduced. However it is his passion for the natural world which has elevated his status to national treasure with an incredible career spanning eight decades. In 1979 he created the epic series *Life on Earth,* which utilised innovative camera techniques to capture stunning photography of animals in their natural habitats including one of the most memorable moments in television history; an encounter with a family of mountain gorillas. He has perhaps done more than anyone else on earth to help millions appreciate the wonders of the natural world.

The Number 78 Bus

An artist's impression of Albert Gunter's extraordinary bus jump

The 30th December 1952 started out as a day like any other for bus driver Albert Gunter. He was a driver on the number 78 bus route from Dulwich to Shoreditch which passed across Tower Bridge. The bridge was completed in 1894 and, at the time, was the most easterly bridge spanning the River Thames. It was designed to split into two sections which would raise when tall boats needed to pass under. By the time that Albert was driving his bus on that fateful day, Tower Bridge had been raised around 300,000 times previously without major incident. There was a series of systems designed to hold traffic back on the approach to the bridge when it was due to be raised. A gateman would ring a warning bell and close the gates and set a signal to red. When the bridge was clear, a watchman would order the bridge to be raised. However, human error meant that as Albert and his bus full of passengers approached, the light was green leading him to think that it was safe to cross. As the bus crossed the bridge it dawned on Albert that it was raising with them on it. With no other option, the quick-thinking driver moved down two gears, slammed on the accelerator, and jumped the 6 foot gap across the water below, landing on the other half of the bridge which luckily was slower to rise. Amazingly, out of the 20 passengers, no one was seriously injured. The bus conductor broke his leg, and an 11-year old boy fractured his collarbone, but the other passengers who were taken to hospital were mainly suffering minor cuts and bruises.

Albert was lauded in the press for his heroics and was given gifts of £10 by London Transport and £35 by the City of London. He was also given a day off work. Albert, though, remained humble about the incident, claiming that he couldn't understand "what the fuss is all about". One of the passengers that day was a Miss May Walshaw, and after the event she was left with a strong fear of travelling by bus. Seven months after the incident, she decided to tackle her fear and undertook the same bus journey across the bridge with Albert as the driver. The journey went without a hitch, and two weeks later May got married, with Albert acting as her best man.

A Hero with Bottle

The Victoria Cross is the highest award in the British Honours System and is awarded for valour "in the presence of the enemy" to members of the British Armed Forces. Awarded by her late father in the previous year, this Victoria Cross was not only the first presented by the new Queen Elizabeth II, it was also one of the most remarkable. The Korean War took place in a divided country. Chinese Communist-backed forces in the North tried to take the South which was backed by Western forces.

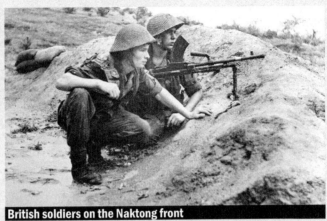
British soldiers on the Naktong front

Private Bill Speakman

In early November 1952 in one of many large-scale attacks by the Chinese, Private Bill Speakman, a Black Watch soldier temporarily attached to the 1st battalion of the King's Own Scottish Borderers, was acting as a runner for B company. He was positioned on a ridge known as Hill 217 where 6,000 Chinese infantry troops were advancing in waves on B Company.

At dusk the company's position looked all but hopeless. However, Speakman, an imposing and well-built man standing 6ft 6in tall, decided otherwise. Filling all available pockets with the hand grenades he had been priming, he rose to his feet. Asked where he thought he was going, Speakman was reported as saying "I'm going to shift some of them bloody Chinese."

Standing in the dark, he pelted the attackers with grenade after grenade, aiming at their rifle flashes, pausing only to return to refill his pockets. Inspired by his actions, six men then joined him in a concerted drive to clear the ridge of the enemy. It seemed that only a bullet could stop Speakman; yet even this was insufficient. He was indeed shot, once in the leg and once in the shoulder. After being patched up, and against medical advice, he returned to the fray. The problem was that he and his comrades had run out of grenades and were reduced to throwing stones, ration tins and even, as legend has it, beer bottles. Eventually pro-Western forces cleared the ridge and Company B could withdraw. The citation for the Victoria Cross stated that he had imposed enormous losses on the enemy and saved the lives of many of his comrades. His medal is on display in the National War Museum of Scotland in Edinburgh Castle.

The Victoria Cross

The Kamchatka Tsunami

50-feet high waves were reported after the magnitude 9.0 earthquake

The Kamchatka Tsunami was caused by a magnitude 9.0 earthquake in Russia's Pacific East Coast. The local tsunami, which generated waves 50-feet high, caused extensive damage to the Kamchatka Peninsula and the nearby Kuril Islands. Tragically, 15,000 people lost their lives. Giant waves also travelled as far as Chile, Peru and New Zealand. In Alaska, the Aleutian Islands and California waves up to 5 feet high were observed. But the largest damage to other parts of the Pacific occurred in the Hawaiian Islands. Much of the infrastructure around the shorelines was swept away including beach huts and a bridge connecting Coconut Island to its neighbour. The largest waves occurred on the north shore of Oahu Island, they were nearly 15-feet high. That Hawaii had a long history of tsunamis stood them in good stead. Six cows were killed, but the human population fled to higher ground until the danger had well and truly passed. The people in the settlement of Severo-Kurilsk in Russia were not so fortunate as three monstrous waves pummelled the shoreline.

Most inhabitants did indeed flee to higher ground when they saw the first wave, but many "thinking that the danger was over" returned to the town before the second wave hit. Four in ten of the townsfolk lost their lives during the second wave and the town was destroyed beyond repair. Severo-Kurilsk was eventually rebuilt in a different location. Tsunami waves can have extremely long wavelengths and warning systems are now in place all around the Pacific "Ring of Fire" coastline. Emergency preparedness professionals now advise evacuees to stay away from the coast until official word that it is safe to return is given.

The port of Severo-Kurlisk where the Tsunami hit

The Washington, D.C. UFO Mass Panic

In the summer of 1952 there were many nights of intense UFO activity over Washington, D.C. From July 12th to July 29th the skies above America's capital seemed to be crowded with UFOs darting here and there, over the White House, the Capitol Building and the Pentagon. They were seen from the ground and also detected on radar from control towers at Washington National Airport, at Bolling Air Force Base across the Potomac River and from nearby Andrews Air Force Base. The radar operators communicated by telephone to ensure they were tracking the same targets. In many cases, airline pilots flying in the area were able to provide visual confirmation of radar tracking. The appearance of unidentified objects flying with impunity over the heart of the American government and its military establishment was embarrassing to the Department of Defence, whose responsibility it was to protect the country from airborne invasion. A flood of questions from reporters led the U.S. Air Force to call its biggest but also most confusing press conference since World War II.

Purported UFO sighting in New Jersey

The conference was held at the Pentagon, and was presided over by Air Force Intelligence Chief, Major General John Samford. The main explanation given for the rash of sightings was something called a "temperature inversion". This can cause mirages but these usually take place on land, not in the skies. General Samford suggested that lights on the ground may have looked like they were in the air because an inversion can act like an "air lens" and bend light rays. He added that something similar could have "tricked" radar into thinking it was tracking aerial targets, which were actually ground objects. This was the first time that this theory had been put forward. It became very useful as an explanation for numerous later cases, though no one in the wider scientific community had heard of this phenomenon. It wasn't until 1969 that an Air Force scientific report made it clear that inversions strong enough to create the effects with which General Samford credited them, could not exist in the earth's atmosphere. Moreover, probably no radar/visual UFO report had ever been caused by a temperature inversion or mirage. The incidents are still a mystery to this day. There remain three plausible explanations. First that the Americans themselves were experimenting with flying saucer technology, secondly that a foreign power was spying on the American capital and thirdly that there was really something out there.

Major General John Samford

The Great London Smog | December 5th to 9th

On December 5th an intense fog descended on London. It was so thick that conductors had to walk in front of their buses holding torches. People in the East End could barely see the pavement beneath them. At first many Londoners were unconcerned as this was a regular winter occurrence since the start of the industrial revolution. The London of the day was a heavily industrialised area.

A policeman controlling traffic in smog-filled Parliament Square

Battersea Power Station

There were several coal-fired power stations situated in the capital's centre, notably at Battersea and Bankside (now Tate Modern). Along with numerous factories, these belched out an almost continuous stream of smoke. Add to this the fact that most homes were heated by the burning of coal and the result would be a toxic mixture, particularly if the atmospheric conditions were conducive to fog. High pressure continued to build holding in the toxins from the pollution which mixed with the moisture in the air. The relatively benign fog became smog; a combination of smoke and fog. Over the next few days the smog pervaded every nook and cranny of the city, even halting indoor events such as theatre and cinema. Just outside London there were even reports of farm animals dying in the fields.

As well as the paralysis brought to city life by people not being able to see and get around, the entire population was breathing in nothing short of poison. It is estimated that 4,000 people died as a direct result of the smog and many thousands more had their lives shortened by the long-term health effects brought about by the incident. On 9th December the high pressure relented, lower pressure brought winds which dispersed the smog and London could breathe again. Parliament decided that something had to be done. After much opposition from vested interests, a Clean Air Act was eventually passed in 1956. This placed restrictions on what could be burnt but it did not entirely solve the problem as there were several more "pea-souper" events, though none as severe as the one Great Smog of 1952.

Nelson's Column in the smog

The Harrow and Wealdstone Train Crash

Emergency services arrived to an horrific scene of utter carnage

The day in this corner of North London started like many others. The affluent suburb of Harrow was shrouded in a thick fog and there was a definite chill in the air. Many residents put on their overcoats and, with briefcase and umbrella in hand, made their way to the station to start the daily commute into the city centre. The fog would play a key part in the disaster that was to follow. The driver of a high-speed train from Perth missed a caution signal that would have instructed him to slow down. The driver missed two more signals and by the time his train was approaching the station it was too late to act. When the Perth train came speeding into the station, it crashed into the rear of a Tring to Euston train that had been held at the station due to the fog. It completely destroyed the rear three coaches of the Euston service, shunting the entire train twenty yards forward. Yet the chaos was not to end here. The leading carriages of the Perth train then piled up onto one another, in so doing spreading the carnage over onto the adjacent line where another train, this one a Euston to Liverpool service, collided with it at some sixty miles per hour, catapulting it into the nearby footbridge.

By the time the dust had settled dozens were already dead and hundreds were in need of medical assistance. The carnage gave rise to several acts of heroism. The most famous of these was Lieutenant Abbie Sweetwine who, after her actions on the day, was dubbed the 'Angel of Platform 6'. As part of a US Air Force medical unit which had been based at RAF Northolt, Sweetwine and the rest of her unit came to Harrow and Wealdstone to help the emergency services in rescuing the trapped and saving the wounded. At the station, Sweetwine was seen comforting the survivors of the day, handing out cigarettes and tea whilst simultaneously tending to the injured earning her angel moniker. Amongst the horror and devastation on that day her uplifting story was widely reported in local and national papers. When the station was finally cleared it was revealed that 112 people had perished and 340 were injured, with 88 being detained in hospital. A memorial plaque for the disaster was unveiled in 2002 to mark the 50th anniversary. A mural by local schoolchildren featuring scenes from Wealdstone's history was also dedicated to the memory of the victims.

The Lynmouth Flood | August 15th and 16th

On a Friday evening in North Devon a small coastal village suffered what could be described as the worst flood in English history. The summer had been unseasonably wet; six inches of rain had fallen in the previous two weeks. Nearby Exmoor which acts like a sponge was saturated. On the day of the flood three inches of rain fell in the morning leading Exmoor to become overwhelmed. When a further six inches fell in the late afternoon the moor was unable to absorb any more water. A local author, S. H. Burton, noted that water stood at a foot and a half on the edge of the moor. The road between Lynmouth and Simonsbath was washed away at a place somewhat ironically called Dry Bridges.

An aerial view of Lynmouth capturing the devastation
Image credit: Julian Gurney/ Lyn Valley History Facebook group

The force of the water and rubble destroyed houses
Image: Tony Bawden. Credit: Julian Gurney/ Ruth Bowden

It has been estimated that nearly 100 million tons of water fell in North Devon and West Somerset that day. Given that the ground was already saturated there was only one place it could go, downhill towards the sea. Lynmouth was in its path. On its way the water met resistance from several bridges before they were swept away. This created a wall not only of water, but also thousands of tons of rubble hurtling towards the village. It arrived during the night. When daylight broke the true horror of the flood was revealed. 34 people lost their lives, with a further 420 made homeless. 100 buildings were destroyed or severely damaged and 28 of the 31 bridges in the area were either lost or rendered impassable.

It took six years to rebuild and remodel the village. A flood defence system designed to cope with rainfall heavier than that which fell in 1952 was put in place to divert water around Lynmouth. A small group of houses on the bank of the East Lyn River in the Hamlet of Middleham just outside Lynmouth were destroyed and never rebuilt. Instead a memorial garden dedicated to all who lost their lives, homes and livelihoods stands on the site.

Richard Haynes's parents recover items from their shop which was almost completely submerged by debris washed down by the raging waters
Credit: Richard Haynes from his book "My Family survived a Disaster" / Aspect-Design Malvern

Saving Lives At Sea | The North Foreland

On a bleak midwinter's night and in almost total darkness the barge Vera ran aground in the Thames Estuary. In heavy seas and with winds gusting up to 50mph, the crew launched two distress flares. In response Her Majesty's Coastguard called the nearest lifeboat station which was at Southend-on-Sea, only to learn that they were already out on another rescue. They then called the next two nearest stations, again to be told that they, too, were out on "shouts." In desperation they contacted Margate which was over 20 miles from the stricken vessel. Despite the distance to travel, the conditions and the fact that they were heading into unfamiliar waters, the brave volunteers did not hesitate to take the call and launched at 3.10 am.

Artist's impression of a Thames Barge struggling in heavy seas

Fighting large waves, rain and squalls of sleet, the lifeboat reached the estuary in a gruelling 2½ hours. However, visibility was almost zero and the crew's efforts to locate the barge seemed hopeless. Their luck would change as dawn broke. They spied the submerged vessel's mast which was 2 miles away. As they sped towards it they spotted two figures high up on the mast. It was the two crew members, who had been clinging on for 5 hours. When they got near to the barge the lifeboatmen saw that getting the men down was going to be very difficult in such fierce winds and high seas.

Lifeboatmen braving stormy seas

The lifeboat crew were left with no option but to attempt an extremely bold manoeuvre. Coxswain Denis Price drove the rescue vessel into the rigging of the barge. He figured that the two men on board could use the rigging to slide down onto the lifeboat. The first man who attempted to slide down missed the lifeboat, but was hauled from the violent sea. The second also looked like he would miss the lifeboat, but quick-thinking Price guided his vessel under the man and he, too, was rescued. The two men were in a bad way, one was close to collapse. The rescuers wrapped them in blankets, gave them food and as was customary in the day, a tot of rum. At 9.45am, six and a half hours after launching, the lifeboat made it back to shore. They docked at Brightlingsea and transferred the two bargemen to the Shipwrecked Mariners' Society, who took care of them from there. In recognition of his bravery and quick-thinking Coxswain Price was awarded the Silver Medal for Gallantry. Second Coxswain Edward Parker and mechanic Alfred Lacey, received a certificate of thanks from the R.N.L.I.

RNLB North Foreland (now retired)

Games of the XV Olympiad | Helsinki Jul 19th – Aug 3rd

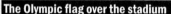

The Olympic flag over the stadium

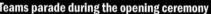

Teams parade during the opening ceremony

Paavo Nurmi lights the flame

The Helsinki Olympics were dubbed the first Cold War Olympics with the rivalry between the Soviet Union and the USA overshadowing the games. The two countries, who had formed an uneasy alliance to defeat Nazi Germany less than a decade earlier, were now the bitterest of enemies. They each saw the Olympics as a means to boost their profile on the world stage while at the same time extolling the supposed superiority of their political systems. Though a record 69 countries took part in the games with over 5000 participants, this was still tiny by comparison with modern Olympiads. It was also the Soviets' first appearance at the games. (The country had participated as Imperial Russia in 1912.)

Soviet input into the games in terms of manpower and resources was immense. Stories were carefully drip-fed by the Russian media of world records being broken in training. The Americans were rightly concerned. The decision of all the Eastern Bloc countries to live in a separate Olympic Village only added to the mystery surrounding them. When it came to the final medals table it was close, with the Americans taking 76 to the Soviets' 71. Back home in Russia the public were treated to a table that showed the two nations tied thanks to a points system that gave great weight to silver medals awarded. The Soviets were even placed top on alphabetical order; lies, damned lies and statistics!

Athletes in the 1500 metres heats

Competing in the long jump

The packed Olympic Stadium

Games of the XV Olympiad | Helsinki Jul 19th – Aug 3rd

Finland versus Mexico basketball match

Emil Zapotek leading the 5000m

Jean Boiteux's 400m win in the pool

Britain had little to show for their efforts. They were not the well-honed Team GB of today, and were playing by a different set of rules from the well-resourced Americans and Russians. They had to wait until the last day of competition to pick up their solitary gold when Harry Llewellyn, Duggie Stewart and Wilf White won the Equestrian Jumping Team Competition.

The star of the Olympiad was neither an American nor a Soviet. It was a 29 year-old captain in the Czech army with the most ungainly running action. Running as if he was about to fall over or that each step might be his last, Emil Zatopek won a unique treble taking 5,000m 10,000m and the Marathon. He had never run a marathon before and during the race had to check with British runner Jim Peters whether he was pacing it right. Jim assured him that he was and Zatopek won the race by over 2 ½ minutes in a World Record time of 2hrs 23mins. After the race Zatopek bypassed the gathering media and went off to his room for a well deserved nap. Whilst Zatopek's unique achievement made him the person of the games, it was probably not the greatest sporting feat. Lis Hartel, who had been paralysed by an attack of polio aged 23, won a silver medal in the equestrian dressage event. Though she was able to regain some muscle use above the knee through intensive physiotherapy, she was still unable to mount or dismount her horse on her own. In one of the greatest and most moving shows of camaraderie in Olympic history Henry Saint Cyr of Sweden, who narrowly beat her for gold, lifted Hartel from her horse to the podium for the medal ceremony.

Lis Hartel riding Jubilee

An Israeli high jumper

1,2,3 for USA in 3m Springboard

Association Football 1952

Two years after England's humiliation at the 1950 World Cup at the hands of footballing minnows the USA, the team returned to the more familiar surroundings of the Home Internationals. These were played between England, Wales, Scotland and Ireland. This time around Wales and England shared the spoils, with both teams garnering two victories after drawing at Ninian Park, Cardiff. Welsh fans will point out that if the modern use of goal difference were employed they would have been champions.

Welsh striker Trevor Ford

Man Utd manager, Matt Busby

The domestic season in England saw Manchester United crowned champions, beating Tottenham Hotspur by 4 points. It was the first time the term "Busby Babes" was used by the media. The manager, Matt Busby, who had led the team to FA Cup success four years previously, was in the process of clearing out dead wood and replacing it with raw young talent. Young guns such as Jackie Blanchflower, Roger Byrne and Mark Jones would soon become household names. The player who was probably the best of the lot, Duncan Edwards, was being nurtured in the youth team. Of the four footballers mentioned three were to lose their lives six years later in the Munich Air Disaster. Only Blanchflower survived, but injuries sustained in the crash curtailed his career. In Scotland, Hibernian won the league with Glasgow Rangers placed second. Glasgow Celtic finished in 9th place. In spite of only finishing 7th in the league, Motherwell won the cup beating Dundee in the final.

In the F.A. Cup Jorge (George) Robledo, one half of a potent Chilean strike force, scored the only goal of the game in the dying minutes of the final to help Newcastle United beat Arsenal. They became the first team to retain the cup since Blackburn some 60 years earlier. So prolific were the South American duo that Newcastle finished the league season with 98 goals, but so leaky was their defence that they only finished in eighth place.

Newcastle Utd celebrating their win

Newcastle about to score at home

Tennis

When Maureen Connolly burst onto the scene in 1951 nobody had seen tennis like it before. Though not without grace, Connolly brought amazing power and intensity to the game allied with a composure that belied her years. Standing at 5 feet 5 inches she acquired the nickname "Little Mo", which compared her to the firepower of "Big Mo" (the nickname for the USS Missouri), which was the US Navy's leading battleship of the day. 1951 saw her win the US Championship and in 1952 she added the Wimbledon crown to her defence of the US title. As she did not compete in the Australian nor the French, this gave her a 100% record. The next year she decided to go for all four. Wimbledon, the US and the Australian were all played on grass, whilst the French took place on clay. All surfaces and all-comers came alike to "Little Mo" as she won all four finals in straight sets, thus becoming the first woman to win the Grand Slam. There was a tragic irony to Connolly's life. As a teenager her first passion was horse riding; she only took up tennis when her single mother told her that they could not afford to keep a horse. As a reward for her success, a neighbour bought her a horse. Aged just 19 she suffered a terrible accident when a concrete truck collided with her horse and she suffered a compressed fracture to her right fibula. The injury finished her career. Though she eventually won compensation for the accident, the world had been deprived of one of the greatest tennis players to grace the game.

Teenage tennis star, Maureen Connolly

In men's tennis Australian Frank Sedgman was the most successful player, reaching all four Grand Slam finals. He won Wimbledon and the US Championship, but lost the French and Australian.

In the Davis Cup, the men's international team championship, the Great Britain team led by team captain Colin Gregory progressed to the quarter finals of the European Zone after a 3-2 victory over Yugoslavia. Their hopes were soon dashed when they were convincingly beaten by Italy. America won the main competition but under the Challenge Cup rules of the day had to play last year's winners Australia for the cup outright. Playing at home the Australians were easy winners, four rubbers to one.

Australian number one, Frank Sedgman

Rugby League

As it is today, 13 a-side rugby league was in 1952 principally played in Lancashire and Yorkshire. There was a short-lived venture by a team from Cardiff to extend the code's reach outside of its traditional homeland. Low attendances at their Penarth Road stadium coupled with a poor season (31 losses out of 36 games) saw them fold before the next season. Bradford Northern finished top of the championship by two points from Wigan; Hull and Huddersfield finished third and fourth. As today the four would go into a series of play-offs. First played fourth with second playing third in the two semi-finals. Thirteen proved to be the lucky number for Wigan as they first beat Hull 13-9 and then overcame Bradford Northern 13-6 in the Grand Final. On April 19th Workington beat Featherstone Rovers 18-10 in the Challenge Cup Final at Wembley in front of a crowd of over 72,000. The season also saw the twelfth staging of the European Rugby League Championship. It was rather a strange concoction with teams from England, Wales and France competing. They were joined by a cobbled together team of overseas players, who played in Britain, which went by the name Other Nationalities. Rugby League is a sport where playing at home is a great advantage. Each side played the others only once and when France was drawn to play England in Marseilles they became firm favourites for the title. They did not disappoint, running out 42-13 winners, cheered on by a crowd of 31,000 in the decisive match of the championship.

Rugby Union

International matches in Rugby League were always seen as secondary to the club game. In Rugby Union it was more the other way around.

The Rugby Union County Championship was England's premier competition of the time and its 52nd edition was won by Middlesex who beat Lancashire in the final.

The French National Rugby Union team

The Five Nations Championship between England, Ireland, Scotland, Wales and France was the one that drew the attention and the crowds. The season was marked by low scoring, physical and grinding games. The last two matches featured no tries at all with England beating Ireland 3-0 at Twickenham and France 6-3 away at the Stade Olympique. By then though the Championship was already decided as Wales, led by legendary captain John Gwilliam, had sealed their fourth win a week earlier when they beat France 9-5. This gave them not only the title but also the Grand Slam. The season also saw the visit of South Africa, the Springboks, who played a mixture of club and international matches. The highlight of a highly successful tour was their first meeting with the Barbarians which saw them convincing winners at Cardiff Arms Park by 17 to 3. The Springboks swept all before them save for a shock 9-11 loss to London Counties. They finished the tour winning 30 out of 31 games.

Cricket

Bowling figures of 1/14 in the match, 3 runs with the bat in the first innings and 19 in the second. These were hardly the most earth-shattering figures but they heralded the arrival of Richie Benaud on to the cricket world stage. For the next twelve years he developed into a fine all-rounder and a superb captain. However after his retirement in 1964, he would became one of sport's greatest commentators. Fleet of mind and sharp of tongue, he was the voice of cricket for a generation.

In the domestic game, Surrey won their eighth county championship, starting what would be an extraordinary run of seven straight titles. It was little wonder that the team dominated the league as it was brim full of talent in every department of the game. Eric Bedser, Bernie Constable and David Fletcher amassed runs in nearly every game, whilst Jim Laker, Tony Lock and Alec Bedser all ripped through the opposition with the ball. It is even more remarkable that they did this without their most promising youngster Peter May, who took a year out to complete his degree at Cambridge University.

In Test cricket, England had a fairly routine 3-0 victory against India. The Indians, who were on their first tour of England since independence, arrived with high hopes. However, conditions favoured the hosts and hopes were soon dashed. The England team of Hutton, Trueman, Graveney and Alec Bedser were simply too strong for the Indians, whose stars included Manjrekar, Phadkar and Mankad. Eagle-eyed aficionados of the game will have noticed the name Mankad. Five years previously, he was involved in one of the most controversial incidents in cricket history. Whilst Mankad was bowling, the Australian batsman at the non-strikers end, Bill Brown, left his crease early in anticipation of a quick single. Mankad halted his run-up and removed the bails. The umpire raised his finger and signalled out. Though the decision was correct, it was felt that it was not within the spirit of the game. Since then similar actions are referred to as Mankading and are still generally frowned upon.

Richie Benaud

The Bedser twins - Eric (left) and Alec (right)

The Grand National

The 106th renewal of The Grand National took place at Aintree racecourse on April 5th. The race featured one of the greatest shocks in its long history. After a false start it went off ten minutes late and was won by Teal, ridden by Arthur Thompson at odds of 100/7 (14 to 1 in today's money.) No shock there then. Leading up to the race, Aintree racecourse was in dispute with the BBC about rights. The head of the racecourse, Mirabel Topham, decided to bring the commentary in-house: "What could go wrong commentating on a 47-runner race over 4 miles and 514 yards", she figured? The shocking thing was that the in-house commentator incorrectly announced that Teal had fallen at the first fence, leading some to tear up their betting slips. Topham found out the hard way. The dispute was eventually settled.

The Derby

The Derby was less eventful and was run on Wednesday 28th May. (Wednesday was the traditional day for the Derby and was not moved to Saturday until 1995.) The winner, Tulyar, was ridden by Charlie Smirke and owned by the Aga Khan. It beat 32 rivals by ¾ of a length and came in at odds of 11/2.

A young Lester Piggott, who was to become the greatest Derby jockey of all time, came second on Gay Time at odds of 25/1.

Lester Piggott (pictured) came 2nd on Gay Time

Greyhound Racing

Greyhound racing was immensely popular in the 1950s with crowds totalling over 50 million attending race meetings in 1952. Racing greyhounds around a track as opposed to the traditional hare coursing, had been introduced from America in the mid-1920s; its quick-fire action was the perfect medium for gambling. The pinnacle of the greyhound racing year was the Derby run at White City, London. Rumours swirled around for months before the race that expert trainer Leslie Reynolds had a wonder dog with punters were advised to fill their boots. The dog, the appropriately named Endless Gossip, did not disappoint by romping home ten lengths ahead. At odds of Even Money (double your stake) it is doubtful anyone got rich, though it might have covered the bar bill.

Greyhound Racing was hugely popular in the 1950s

The 1952 World Snooker Tournament

25th February to 8th March 1952
Venue: Houldsworth Hall, Manchester

The 1952 World Snooker tournament was the most farcical event in this or any other sport. The governing body determined that Snooker should be more about honour than financial reward. However, nearly all the players begged to differ. This left a field of two, the Australian Horace Lindrum and the New Zealander Clarke McConarchy. It was decided that they would play one match over an astonishing 145 frames, meaning that the first to 73 would win. Lindrum lead 42-28 after a gruelling week's play. By the ninth day he had stretched his lead to 61-35. By March 6th Lindrum went into an unassailable lead of 73-37. Astonishingly they decided to play on with the champion winning 94-49 before randomly calling it a day, two frames short of the scheduled 145. Maybe they had something better to do? Who said Steve Davis was boring! Lindrum is, however, recognised as the first overseas winner of the World Snooker title. Many dispute this as he beat only one other player and they believe that honour falls to Neil Robertson who won in 2010.

Horace Lindrum
(pictured earlier in his career)

1952 Tour of Britain

The Bradford-born Ken Russell may not be as well remembered as the other British sporting greats of the era: Roger Bannister's 4 minute mile in 1954, Jim Laker's 19 wickets in one match in 1956 or Stanley Matthews' cup final feats of 1953, but the cyclist's achievements possibly trumped them all. The second Daily Express Tour of Britain was the greatest cycle race Britain had ever seen. The event finished at London's Alexandra Palace on September 6th and it was won by a man the experts said could not win. The odds were stacked against Russell. He had no team to help him, he was an amateur who worked in a bicycle shop and he finished the race riding a borrowed bike. When news of his impending victory broke, thousands lined the streets for the final 30-mile stage to the palace. Russell finished the stage in second place, but retained the overall lead. He beat professional teams from France, Italy and Belgium, the giants of the sport. His prize money was £140 which, compared to a football player's salary of £10 a week, was good money and it allowed Russell to found his own bicycle sales company.

1,470 miles of racing around Britain

A Sugar High and Sugar Low

It was a mixed year for Sugar Ray Robinson, a man many believe to have been the best pound-for-pound fighter ever to box. On March 15th Robinson defended his World Welterweight title in a bruising 15-round encounter with fellow American Carl "Bobo" Olsen. Although on top for most of the fight, Robinson could not land the killer blow. The judges did, however, return a unanimous verdict and Robinson retained the crown. Things took a turn for the worse when he fought Joey Maxim. Born Guiseppe Antonio Berardinelli, Maxim chose his ring name to reflect the fact that the rapidity of his punches resembled a Maxim machine gun. The fight was held in sweltering heat in New York. It was so hot that even the referee was taken to hospital with heat exhaustion in the tenth round. During the thirteenth round the ringside doctor ordered that the fight be stopped, when the spent and dehydrated Robinson had nothing more to offer. He was also taken to hospital. The verdict was that Robinson lost by a knockout, the only such loss of his career.

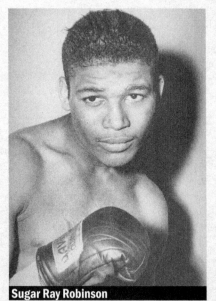
Sugar Ray Robinson

Frank Johnson claims the British Lightweight crown

Frank Johnson is the forgotten man of British boxing. Even fight aficionados struggle to recall his name. Perhaps it was the fact that he fought in the unglamorous lightweight division, or that he never had the chance to fight for a world title. However, his name deserves to be spoken alongside the pantheon of British greats of the sport. His amateur record of 365 fights with only 3 defeats is testimony to his greatness with one leading commentator declaring that Johnson was "the best British boxer I ever saw at any weight." Although Johnson hailed from Manchester, he fought mainly out of the south of England. Finally, on July 25th 1952, the Mancunian returned home to fight Tommy McGovern, in front of his townsfolk, for the British title. Johnson was fleet of foot with fast hands and a knack of working out an opponent. After the full 15 rounds, Johnson was declared the winner by a unanimous decision. The following year saw Johnson become the first Englishman to travel to Australia to fight for the Empire Lightweight title.

Frank Johnson

There he fought the rugged Australian champion and overwhelming favourite Frankie Flannery. Johnson not only won but won convincingly. Leading Aussie commentator Merv Williams declared that Johnson was "the fastest and most accomplished boxer Britain has produced in years." Like many boxers of the era, he fought on past his best and his professional record of 47 wins and 11 losses bears little resemblance to his near flawless amateur record. Still he was one of the greats.

Golf

In 1952 the "Majors", the world's four premier golfing tournaments, consisted of two British and two American events. Britain, being the home of golf, simply called theirs The Open and The Amateur Championship. The Americans held the US Open and the US Amateur. As golf became more professional, The Masters and The PGA (both American tournaments) replaced both amateur championships to form what we now know as the Majors. Britain, and in particular Scotland, may have been the home of golf but America was its bank. The US tour was lucrative, but also a bit of a closed shop at the time. Golfers could earn a decent wage, though nothing by today's standards as sponsorship was in its infancy. Few British golfers made it over to America and few Americans came to Britain, not even for The Open. Prize money for The Open was low (£300) and even if an American won it, he might not cover the cost of his trip. There is also the fact that the two countries played on vastly different courses. The Americans played on well manicured fairways, while the British played on rough and ready links courses. Generally speaking the American golfers relied largely on power, the British on accuracy.

The 1952 (British) Open was the 81st time the tournament was played, and the second time it was held at Royal Lytham & St Annes Golf Club on the Lancashire coast. The champion from 1947, Northern Ireland's Fred Daly, led after the first two days. Back then the final day was a much more severe test as two rounds had to be completed to lift the Claret Jug. The morning began well for Daly, but in increasingly blustery conditions he could only finish with a 5 over par, 77. Two-times previous winner, South African Bobby Locke, had cut Daly's overnight lead from four shots to one. Conditions did improve slightly in the afternoon but Daly was unable to hold his lead. Locke ran out the winner by one shot, holding off a late charge from Australia's Peter Thompson, one of only two of the top 10 players to break par that day. A disconsolate Daly finished only third. Peter Alliss who was to become the voice of golf shot two par rounds on the first two days but faded out of contention.

The USPGA, then held as a match play tournament, was won by Jim Turnesa. The US Masters, held at its traditional home of Augusta, was won by the great Sam Snead and the US Open was claimed by Julius Boros in a four-round score of one over par.

Royal Lytham & St Annes Golf Club

The Open champion Bobby Locke

US golfer Sam Snead

Austin-Healey was a British sports car maker established in 1952 through a joint venture between the Austin division of the British Motor Corporation and the Donald Healey Motor Company. Pictured is a 1953 Austin Healey 100 BN1.

The Austin A40 Somerset built by the Austin Motor Company was launched in 1952. The Somerset included a 1.2 litre straight-4 pushrod engine, producing 42hp which could propel the car to a top speed of 70mph.

The Avro Vulcan, a jet-powered, tailless, delta-wing, high-altitude, strategic bomber, took its maiden test flight on the 30th August 1952. Operated by the RAF it entered service in 1956 until 1984.

The Boeing B-52 Stratofortress, an American long-range, subsonic, jet-powered strategic bomber, took its maiden test flight on 15th April 1952. It would enter service in February 1955 and, remarkably, is still in service today.

The Brownie was a series of cameras made by Eastman Kodak. The Brownie 127 model was launched in 1952 and sold in its millions until it was replaced in 1967. It had a Bakelite body and a simple meniscus lens.

Today known as simply Olay, Oil of Olay originated in South Africa in 1952 led by former Unilever chemist Graham Wulff. He chose the name "Oil of Olay" as a spin on the word "lanolin", a key ingredient.

In 1890 Thomas Tunnock bought a bakery in Uddingston, Scotland for £80 thereby starting the Tunnock's company. In the 1950s his son, Archie, created the 5-layer, caramel wafer biscuit which went on sale to the public in 1952.

"Sugar Frosted Flakes" is a breakfast cereal introduced in the USA by the Kellogg Company in 1952. Tony The Tiger, the cereal's mascot, has been exclaiming "They're Gr-r-reat!" since its introduction. Frosties is the brand name in the UK.

Photo Credits

Credits shown in the order in which they appear in the book. Photos not listed are in the public domain.

Key to page numbers

fc = front cover; **ifc** = inside front cover; **tp** = title page; **cp** = contents page; **ap1** = acknowledgements page 1; **ap2** = acknowledgements page 2; **rop** = reader offer page; **ibc** = inside back cover; **bc** = back cover; **3** = page 3; **4** = page 4; etc.

Key to object position on page

tl = top left; *t* = top; *tc* = top centre; *tr* = top right; *cla* = centre left above; *ca* = centre above; *cra* = centre right above; *cl* = centre left; *c* = centre; *cr* = centre right; *clb* = centre left below; *cb* = centre below; *crb* = centre right below; *bl* = bottom left; *b* = bottom; *bc* = bottom centre; *br* = bottom right; *w* = whole page; *h* = header; *tb* = text background

Key to image licence types

CC BY-SA 2.0 = https://creativecommons.org/licenses/by-sa/2.0/deed.en;
CC BY-SA 3.0 = https://creativecommons.org/licenses/by-sa/3.0/deed.en;
CC BY-SA 4.0 = https://creativecommons.org/licenses/by-sa/4.0/deed.en;
(m) = image has been modified as permitted under licensing terms

Photo Credits continued

76 *tr*: Lighting Flame (m) © Helsinki City Museum, Wikimedia Commons, CC BY-SA 2.0; **76** *bl*: 1500m (m) © Helsinki City Museum, Wikimedia Commons, CC BY-SA 4.0; **76** *bc*: Long jump (m) © Helsinki City Museum, Wikimedia Commons, CC BY-SA 4.0; **76** *br*: Stadium (m) © Helsinki City Museum, Wikimedia Commons, CC BY-SA 4.0; **77** *bc*: High Jump (m) © Fritz Cohen, Wikimedia Commons, CC BY-SA 3.0; **81** *tr*: Richie Benaud © BBC Archive; **82** *cr*: Lester Piggott (m) © Ragge Strand, Bjørn Fjørtoft, Rolf Engesland, Wikimedia Commons, CC BY-SA 4.0; **82** *br*: Greyhound Racing (m) © RJRoweCollection, Wikimedia Commons, CC BY-SA 4.0; **83** *br*: Cycle Race (m) © Helsinki City Museum, Wikimedia Commons, CC BY-SA 4.0; **84** *br*: Frank Johnson (m) © Stevo16star, Wikimedia Commons, CC BY-SA 4.0; **85** *tr*: Royal Lytham & St Annes Clubhouse (m) © G Laird /Royal Lytham & St Annes Golf Club, Wikimedia Commons, CC BY-SA 2.0; **86** *t*: Austin Healey (m) © Sicnag, Wikimedia Commons, CC BY-SA 2.0; **86** *b*: Austin A40 (m) © Vauxford, Wikimedia Commons, CC BY-SA 4.0; **87** *t*: Avro Vulcan (m) © Alastair Barbour, Wikimedia Commons, CC BY-SA 2.0; **88** *t*: Brownie 127 (m) © George Rex, Wikimedia Commons, CC BY-SA 4.0; **88** *b*: Oil of Olay (m) © Procter and Gamble Heritage Center, Wikimedia Commons, CC BY-SA 4.0; **89** *tl*: Tunnocks wrapper (m) © Grinner, Wikimedia Commons, CC BY-SA 2.0; **89** *bl*: Frosted Flakes in bowl (m) © Th78blue, Wikimedia Commons, CC BY-SA 4.0; **89** *bl*: Marble (m) © Yana Iskayeva, Unsplash.com; **92** *tc*: Coffee Table (m) © Sincerely Media, Unsplash.com; **BC** *tr*: Queen Elizabeth at the Chelsea Flower Show (m) © Karen Roe, Flickr, CC BY-SA 2.0.

Graphic and Background Image Credits

Credits shown in the order in which they appear in the book.

Additional Key

(ic) = icon; (ph) = photo

fc *c*, **tp** *ca*, **bc** *w* & **2-15** *w*: (ph) Texture by Felipe Santana, Unsplash; **2-3, 14-92** *tb*: (m)(ph) Paper Texture by rawpixel.com; **3** *cla*: (ic) Play by Adrien Coquet, thenounproject.com, CC BY-SA 2.0; **6,8,10,12,14** & **7,9,11,13,15** *tr*: (ic) Newspaper by Loïc Poivet, thenounproject.com, CC BY-SA 2.0; **6-15** *c*: (ph) Book by Robert Armstrong, Pixabay; **16-25,42-61,86-92** *w*: (m)(ph) Concrete texture by rawpixel.com; **16,18,20,22** *tl* & **17,19,21,23** *tr*: (ic) Birthday Calendar by Kiran Shastry, thenounproject.com, CC BY-SA 2.0; **16** *cla* & **18** *crb*: (ic) Cricket by SANB, thenounproject.com, CC BY-SA 2.0; **16** *clb*: (ic) Space by IronSV, thenounproject.com, CC BY-SA 2.0; **17,19,21** *cla*: (ic) Theatre Comedy by B Farias, thenounproject.com, CC BY-SA 2.0; **17** *clb*: (ic) Mannequin by Blair Adams, thenounproject.com, CC BY-SA 2.0; **18,21** *cla* & **25** *bl*: (ic) Clapper Board by Andrew Nielsen, thenounproject.com, CC BY-SA 2.0; **18,22** *clb*: (ic) Theatre by Ben Davis, thenounproject.com, CC BY-SA 2.0; **19,20** *clb*: (ic) Music Note by Karen Tyler, thenounproject.com, CC BY-SA 2.0; **20** *cla*: (ic) Tennis by Mister Pixel, thenounproject.com, CC BY-SA 2.0; **22** *cla*: (ic) Celebrities by Mrfa Studio, thenounproject.com, CC BY-SA 2.0; **23** *tl*: (ic) Pencil by Alice Design, thenounproject.com, CC BY-SA 2.0; **23** *clb*: (ic) Baby by Emily Keller, thenounproject.com, CC BY-SA 2.0; **24** *tl* & **25** *tr*: (ic) Wreath by Alex Muravev, thenounproject.com, CC BY-SA 2.0; **24** *tl*: (ic) Royal Crown by Vectors Market, thenounproject.com, CC BY-SA 2.0; **24,25** *cl*: (ic) Speaker by popcornarts, thenounproject.com, CC BY-SA 2.0; **24** *bl*: (ic) Doctor by WEBTECHOPS LLP, thenounproject.com, CC BY-SA 2.0; **25** *tl*: (ic) Army by Viral faisalovers, thenounproject.com, CC BY-SA 2.0; **26** *tl* & **27** *tr*: (ic) Coins by Evgenii Likhachov, thenounproject.com, CC BY-SA 2.0; **26-40** *w*: (m)(ph) White Concrete Wall by rawpixel.com; **28** *tl*: (ic) Army by Viral faisalovers, thenounproject.com, CC BY-SA 2.0; **29** *tr*: (ic) Office by Anggara Putra, thenounproject.com, CC BY-SA 2.0; **30** *tl*: (ic) Tractor by Olivier Guin, thenounproject.com, CC BY-SA 2.0; **31** *tr*: (ic) School Desk by Jongrak, thenounproject.com, CC BY-SA 2.0; **32** *tl*: (ic) Exams by Arjan Farzkenari, thenounproject.com, CC BY-SA 2.0; **33** *tr*: (ic) Children by IronSV, thenounproject.com, CC BY-SA 2.0; **34** *tl* & **35** *tr*: (ic) Home by Numero Uno, thenounproject.com, CC BY-SA 2.0; **36** *tl*: (ic) Lamb by monkik, thenounproject.com, CC BY-SA 2.0; **37** *tr*: (ic) Fruit by novani, thenounproject.com, CC BY-SA 2.0; **38** *tl* & **39** *tr*: (ic) Fashion by Mahmure Alp, thenounproject.com, CC BY-SA 2.0; **40** *tl*: (ic) Holiday by Claudia Revalina, thenounproject.com, CC BY-SA 2.0; **41** *tr*: (ic) Christmas Tree by Azam Ishaq, thenounproject.com, CC BY-SA 2.0; **41** *w*: Christmas (m) © Annie Spratt, Unsplash.com; **42** *tl*: (ic) Entertainment by shashank singh, thenounproject.com, CC BY-SA 2.0; **43,45** *tr* & **44** *tl*: (ic) Clapper Board by Andrew Nielsen, thenounproject.com, CC BY-SA 2.0; **46** *tl*: (ic) Radio by GreenHill, thenounproject.com, CC BY-SA 2.0; **47** *tr*: (ic) Old TV by Eko Purnomo, thenounproject.com, CC BY-SA 2.0; **49,50** *tl* & **49** *tr*: (ic) Record by Mourad Mokrane, thenounproject.com, CC BY-SA 2.0; **51** *tr*: (ic) Music Note by Karen Tyler, thenounproject.com, CC BY-SA 2.0; **52** *tl* & **53** *tr*: (ic) Trumpet by Valter Bispo, thenounproject.com, CC BY-SA 2.0; **54** *tl*: (ic) Arts by Kelsey Armstrong, thenounproject.com, CC BY-SA 2.0; **55,56** *tr* & **57** *tl*: (ic) Book by Travis Avery, thenounproject.com, CC BY-SA 2.0; **58** *tl* & **59** *tr*: (ic) Theatre by Ben Davis, thenounproject.com, CC BY-SA 2.0; **60** *tl*: (ic) Sculpture by Creative Mania, thenounproject.com, CC BY-SA 2.0; **61** *tr*: (ic) Poetry by Martin, thenounproject.com, CC BY-SA 2.0; **62,64** *tl*: (ic) Thinking by Fiona OM, thenounproject.com, CC BY-SA 2.0; **63** *tr*: (ic) Airplane by Matthew S Hall, thenounproject.com, CC BY-SA 2.0; **65** *tr*: (ic) Earth by Natalia Woodroffe, thenounproject.com, CC BY-SA 2.0; **66** *tl*: (ic) Apple by DinosoftLab, thenounproject.com, CC BY-SA 2.0; **67** *tr*: (ic) Genius by Icons Producer, thenounproject.com, CC BY-SA 2.0; **68** *tl*: (ic) Bus by A184, thenounproject.com, CC BY-SA 2.0; **68** *w*: Tower Bridge (m) © Martin Falbisoner, Wikimedia Commons, CC BY-SA 3.0; **69** *tr*: (ic) Medal by Aleksandr Vector, thenounproject.com, CC BY-SA 2.0; **68** *w*: Memorial (m) © Lorie Shaull, Wikimedia Commons, CC BY-SA 2.0; **70** *tl*: (ic) Tsunami by Peter van Driel, thenounproject.com, CC BY-SA 2.0; **70** *w*: Rough Sea (m) © César Couto, Unsplash; **71** *tr*: (ic) UFO by Chanut is Industries, thenounproject.com, CC BY-SA 2.0; **71** *w*: Alien (m) © Stephen Leonardi, Unsplash; **72** *tl*: (ic) Big Ben by Carpe Diem, thenounproject.com, CC BY-SA 2.0; **72** *w*: Fog (m) © Annie Spratt, Unsplash; **73** *tr*: (ic) Train by Sierra Pennala, thenounproject.com, CC BY-SA 2.0; **73** *w*: Platform (m) © Charles Forerunner, Unsplash; **74** *tl*: (ic) Rain by Andi Nur Abdillah, thenounproject.com, CC BY-SA 2.0; **74** *w*: Lynmouth (m) © John-Mark Strange, Unsplash; **75** *tr*: (ic) Life Ring by Made, thenounproject.com, CC BY-SA 2.0; **75** *w*: Sea (m) © Matt Hardy, Unsplash; **76** *tl* & **77** *tr*: (ic) Olympic Rings by sachan, thenounproject.com, CC BY-SA 2.0; **76** *w*: Athletics Race (m) © Braden Collum, Unsplash.com; **77** *w*: Stadium (m) © Helsinki City Museum, Wikimedia Commons, CC BY-SA 4.0; **78** *tl*: (ic) Football by leo-graph.com, thenounproject.com, CC BY-SA 2.0; **78** *w*: Football Pitch (m) © Alberto Frías, Unsplash.com; **79** *tr*: (ic) Tennis by Mister Pixel, thenounproject.com, CC BY-SA 2.0; **78** *w*: Tennis Court (m) © M. Z., Unsplash.com; **80** *tl*: (ic) Rugby Ball by Marco Livolsi, thenounproject.com, CC BY-SA 2.0; **80** *w*: Rugby Match (m) © Alex Motoc, Unsplash.com; **80** *h*: Rugby Lineout © Auckland Museum, Wikimedia Commons, CC BY-SA 4.0; **81** *tr*: (ic) Cricket by Bernd Lakenbrink, thenounproject.com, CC BY-SA 2.0; **81** *w*: Cricketer (m) © Yogendra Singh, Unsplash.com; **82** *tl*: (ic) Horse Racing by Sergio Morozov, thenounproject.com, CC BY-SA 2.0; **82** *w*: Horse Race (m) © Luisa Peter, Unsplash.com; **82** *h*: Horse Race (m) © Jongsun Lee, Wikimedia Commons, CC BY-SA 3.0; **83** *tr*: (ic) Snooker by Phạm Thanh Lộc, thenounproject.com, CC BY-SA 2.0; **83** *tr*: (ic) Cycling by Monika, thenounproject.com, CC BY-SA 2.0; **83** *h*: Snooker © DerHexer, Wikimedia Commons, CC BY-SA 4.0; **83** *h*: Cycling © Fritz Cohen, Flickr, CC BY-SA 3.0; **83** *b*: Cycle Race (m) © Quino Al, Unsplash.com; **84** *tl*: (ic) Boxing Glove by Anton Anuchin, thenounproject.com, CC BY-SA 2.0; **84** *w*: Boxing Match (m) © Johann Walter Bantz, Unsplash.com; **85** *tr*: (ic) Golfing by Nicolas Vicent, thenounproject.com, CC BY-SA 2.0; **85** *w*: Golfing (m) © Courtney Cook, Unsplash.com; **85** *h*: Golf Ball (m) © mk. s, Unsplash.com; **86,88** *tl* & **87,89** *tl*: (ic) Framed Picture by Lil Squid, thenounproject.com, CC BY-SA 2.0; **90** *tl* & **91** *tr*: (ic) Camera by AomAm, thenounproject.com, CC BY-SA 2.0; **92** *tl*: (ic) Present by Vinzence Studio, thenounproject.com, CC BY-SA 2.0

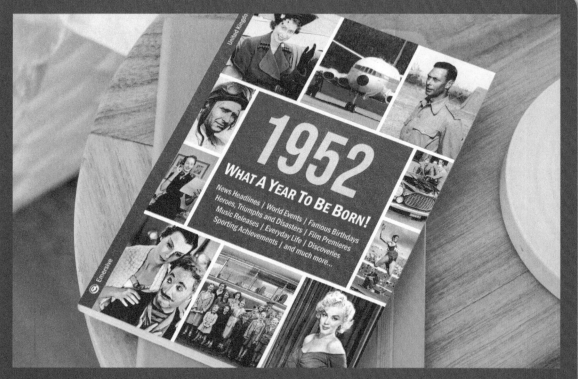
Answers to the Eleven-plus Exam on page 32

Arithmetic Questions

Q1: The motorist has travelled 202 miles

Q2: 314

Q3: The ship could travel 120 miles

Q4: Four hundred and sixty five

Q5: A) Elizabeth's father was 36 years old

Q5: B) In 7 years' time

Q5: C) Elizabeth will be 30 years old

General Intelligence Questions

Q1: A) **Billy** was stung by **a** bee.

Q1: B) The shepherd **stood** by the gate and **whistled** to his dog.

Q1: C) The **family** went to the pool for a **swim**.

Q2: A) Coconut

Q2: B) Giraffe

Q2: C) Patricia

Q3: A) When the dog saw me, it wagged **its** tail.

Q3: B) The subject doesn't concern you or **me**.

Q3: C) Whilst speaking to my brother, the police car **passed** me.